IMAGES OF PEACE

a television chronicle of a turning point in history

CBS Television Network

22453

22453

FOREWORD: *Broadcasting is many different things, but above all it is the act of creating images. At first through sound alone, and later through the combination of sound, sight and motion, it has been implanting images in the minds of multitudes of people for more than three decades—images of themselves and the objective world in which they live, as well as images of their aspirations, of the kind of world in which they would like to live.*

Over the past twenty years none of these images has been as compelling or as elusive as the image of peace. As broadcasters throughout this period we have tried to discern, reproduce and communicate this image whenever and wherever it has shown enough of its face to be identified and seen. We have done this in the belief that by revealing even its dimmest outlines we could help to crystallize its reality. We have followed it with microphone and camera through two wars and from one international conference to another — from Potsdam to San Francisco to Geneva, even to Moscow.

On August 3, 1959, the image of peace seemed to acquire a sudden sharpness of definition with the announcement of President Eisenhower's decision to visit Western Europe, to invite the Soviet Premier to the United States and to visit in return the Soviet Union. Once again we packed our bags and instruments. Here are some of the images we found, brought back, and transmitted to the American people.

THE VIEW FROM EUROPE

By the time CBS News correspondents Charles Collingwood and Robert Pierpoint, along with 44 other journalists, boarded the Presidential Press plane bound for Bonn on August 26, 1959, it was amply clear that for television there could be no half-way measures.

From the moment President Eisenhower stepped on the carpeted platform at Wahn Airport, the implications of his mission for the welfare of mankind were charged with such significance as to require television's all-out coverage. For television this kind of coverage was inherently more demanding than for a newspaper, since it couldn't be confined merely to assigning a reporter equipped with a notebook, waiting for his story to arrive, and then giving it the space it deserved.

With television the job was somewhat more complex. For one thing it meant providing specific time periods for the news programs in a broadcast schedule that was already filled to capacity nearly 18 hours of the day. (A newspaper can merely increase the number of its pages.) This meant the pre-emption of regularly scheduled network and local programs—a practice that is not uniformly applauded by viewers devoted to watching their favorite programs at an accustomed time. To be practicable, such pre-emptions had to be scheduled in time to inform the viewer in advance. Hence the necessity for what may sometimes have appeared to be an inordinately elaborate process—the process of electronically reporting events that took place across 3000 miles of ocean within a 24-hour span—*on schedule.*

Apart from the essential barriers of language and custom, there were the imposing hurdles of foreign and unfamiliar operating procedures, personnel and technical equipment. It meant relaying the television picture by microwave and cable through four different countries, and then reconciling the electronic standards of three different European television systems. It meant recording these pictures on video tape in time

West Germans waiting for Eisenhower's arrival

Video tape recording console

for the departure of jet planes from England to the United States.

There was, to be sure, a body of experience to fall back on—the successful transatlantic coverage of two coronations—those of Queen Elizabeth II and Pope John XXIII. But each of these events had begun and ended in a single day, as opposed to the President's prospective 11-day journey to Europe and the 12-day American visit of Premier Khrushchev.

At the same time, there was little doubt that the problems, though considerable, could be solved. Following the White House announcement of the two visits, the real question that faced the group of men gathered at CBS News headquarters to determine television's course of action over the ensuing weeks could perhaps only be answered after the events themselves: Was it worth it?

Obviously the American people could get their information speedily and simply from radio. Moreover, since the events would be fully covered by every important newspaper in the world, people would be able to read a complete account of each day's developments. They would even get plenty of pictures to look at.

The men at CBS News did not contend that television could do a better job than the older media. But they did believe it could do a *different* job. It could provide an additional dimension of information about this new departure in international diplomacy.

It could enable people to become eyewitnesses to history in the making—and by transporting the viewer in time and space to where it was being made—enable him to become a participant in the process. Through the medium's matchless ability to reveal the nature of human personality, millions of people could get a deeper understanding of the character and motives of the statesmen involved. This collective experience was one that only television could offer—and that only a television network could make available simultaneously to a nationwide audience.

In these circumstances it clearly seemed worth doing.

On Tuesday, August 25—the day before Collingwood and Pierpoint departed—CBS News had issued a 21-page over-all plan for coverage of the events. It was as elaborate, detailed and precise as a battle plan, and like any broadcasting venture—until air time—completely tentative.

The two correspondents would accompany President Eisenhower throughout the entire trip. Sharing with them the task of reporting and analyzing the events were the staffs of the CBS News Bureaus in Germany, England and France—headed by Ernest Leiser in Bonn, Alexander Kendrick in London, and David Schoenbrun in Paris. Don Hewitt who had directed the two coronation broadcasts was designated producer-director of the overseas unit and Foreign Editor Ralph Paskman, overseas coordinator. Assistant CBS News Director Malcolm Johnson and Executive Producer Paul Levitan would be responsible for supervision and production of coverage at headquarters in New York.

The key to the entire venture lay in the relatively new and revolutionary technique of video tape recording—a process that enables the television picture to be reproduced at the same time that it is being broadcast. Although used extensively in this country for nearly two years, tape recording was later introduced in Europe by the British Granada Television Network, the organization which had also perfected the most successful and efficient technique to date of converting the varying signal standards of different European television systems.

At 7:19 pm on August 11 a message in traditional cablese went out from Johnson in New York to Kendrick in London:

CURRENT PLANNING ON EISENHOWER CALLS FOR WEST GERMAN TELEVISION TO COVER IKE ARRIVAL LIVE BONN TRANSMITTING COVERAGE TO ENGLAND FOR VIDEO TAPING BY GRANADA FOR RELAY BY JET TO NEW YORK STOP GRANADA SAYS WILL MOVE PORTABLE VIDEO TAPE RECORDER TRANSLATOR TO DOVER OR LONDON AIRPORT FOR 500 POUNDS WHICH OKAY STOP PLEASE CHECK OUT TIME SAVING WISE WHETHER WE BETTER OFF PUT PORTABLE DOVER WHERE ABLE BYPASS CONVERSION TO 405 LINES AND TRANSLATE DIRECTLY TO 525 AND CARRY FINISHED TAPE BY HELICOPTER TO LONDON JET LINER AIRPORT OR FASTER IF PUT PORTABLE AT AIRPORT QUERY WHAT GRANADA WOULD CHARGE DAILY

OR WEEKLONG BASIS FOR USE THEIR PORTABLE RECORDER AND APPROPRIATE OPERATING PERSONNEL AS WE MAY WANT FULLEST USE THIS UNIT TO RECORD LIVE SPECIAL EVENTS PROGRAMMING ON EISENHOWER AS BROADCAST BY ASSOCIATED REDIFFUSION AND BBC IF LATTER PERMISSIBLE.

The message further suggested that Kendrick inquire whether British television equipment and crews could be sent to Bonn to backstop any possible failure of West German television in covering the President's arrival. It also informed Kendrick that both Hewitt and Paskman would be in London for two days before proceeding to Bonn to participate in the broadcast of the President's arrival, after which they would return to London for the British phase of the news coverage.

The reference to the portable "translator" concerned the all-important problem of signal conversion. West German television operates on a 625-line standard; French television on 819 lines; British on 405, and American on a 525-line standard. An even more complicating factor: European electric power operates at a 50-cycle rate; American at 60 cycles. Before Americans could see a German-originated picture it had to be converted or "translated" into the American standard.

Kendrick's reply clearly indicated the desirability of locating the converter at London Airport where it could receive the picture by microwave relay and telephone line from Germany, convert it directly to the American 525-line standard, and record it on video tape. Transatlantic jet and piston planes would then fly the finished tape to Idlewild Airport in New York.

This, basically, was the established technique for all transmission, the same procedures applying to subsequent broadcasts originating in France and England.

A similar system—minus the conversion process—was set up at Idlewild. A specially built CBS News truck, housing a miniature broadcasting studio and containing camera, video tape recording and transmitting equipment, was strategically located at a point nearest the landing strips of the Pan American and BOAC planes. Known as the CBS

4

News remote mobile unit, it could originate video tape recordings, or monitor, edit and beam the incoming tapes to the microwave receiving dish atop the Empire State Building transmitter. From there the picture would be sent to Master Control at CBS Television Network headquarters, and thence out to the nationwide audience.

At the same time a short wave radio communications unit was set up in the CBS Central News Room in the Grand Central Building. This could be used to maintain direct contact with the remote unit at Idlewild, Master Control, the main Video Tape Recording Room, and whatever television studio a particular program might be coming out of.

It was the switchboard through which all communications passed between CBS News engineers, producers, directors, traffic supervisors, and studio technicians. At any point information could be obtained or instructions transmitted concerning the arrival or delay of planes, the quality of the incoming video tape pictures, and the second-by-second broadcast content of the network schedule. It was a useful gadget.

During the days immediately preceding the President's departure for Bonn, the CBS News traffic department worked out the complicated transatlantic plane schedules essential to the success of the venture. A huge blackboard timetable in the Central News Room posted the daily arrival of planes carrying tapes and films from overseas as well as other flights carrying "safety" duplicates of the original tape and film in the event of a breakdown along the line.

Although the flight schedule was prepared with painstaking detail, it still remained only a blueprint up to the day of the President's arrival in Germany. The big question was — would it work? The only way to find out was to try.

At 10:15 am (British time) on the morning of August 26 CBS News launched a "dry-run" in which the key equipment was put to the test. As a stiff wind swept over London Airport, two engineers stood in front of a television camera and spoke into a microphone:

HARKER: Hello CBS. This is Don Harker of Granada TV talking to you from

West German television camera

Posting plane schedules, CBS Central Newsroom

Camera platform and press scaffolding, Wahn Airport

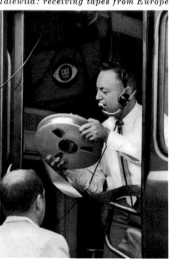

Idlewild: receiving tapes from Europe

CBS News Mobile broadcasting unit at Idlewild

London Airport. We're down here from Manchester with our traveling eye outside broadcast vans, our mobile video tape machines, our eagle towers, and last, but certainly not least on this occasion, our Granada converter. This is the first trial run in a venture, an exciting venture, for us at any rate, in which we hope to bring to you the pictures that you want of President Eisenhower's visit here and we hope to get them to you in the time you want, which means hustling along a bit. What's happening is roughly this: I'm talking to you now and the time is about 10:15 am on a bright morning, a particularly bright morning for Britain, and as soon as I finish talking to you the tape will be taken from the converter and rushed around by courier to the far side of the airport, about 3 miles away, where a Boeing 707 jet airliner will be waiting to carry it to you across the Atlantic. There will be a few passengers as well, of course. This process of conversion is taking place in a van only about 50 yards away. It's an interesting process and I think it would be a good idea to hear about it from our technical supervisor on this operation, Ron Greenough, who's with me. Ron, over to you.

Microwave relay post, Wahn Airport

GREENOUGH: Thank you very much, Don. Don was a bit worried about using this lip mike but as you saw at the start of this, we have aircraft landing and taking off only a few hundred feet away from this camera position, so the use of the lip mike is absolutely essential... This camera is being controlled from a mobile video tape vehicle which is a standard scanner. It has been developed by Granada engineers to hold two mobile cameras plus a video tape recording machine which has been slightly modified to get into the vehicle. The vision and sound from that vehicle is being fed into another similar-size vehicle alongside which has a complete conversion unit. This converts the pictures from British 405-50 cycle standards to the American 525-60 cycles, and for this we have had to bring down to London Airport a 50-cycle converter. So far everything seems to be working well and we hope that this will continue for all the programs that Granada is doing for CBS throughout the visit of the President of the U. S. to Europe. Well, I think we've done a good 5 or 6 minutes of this test tape now, and so I'll sign off and hope that CBS of America gets this tape in good time.

That same afternoon in New York, from the control room of Studio 44, Executive Producer Levitan puts in a call over the intercom to Vern Diamond, in charge of the mobile unit at Idlewild. Levitan was monitoring a series of audio and video checks on a test pattern transmitted by the unit. He wants to get the latest report on the London test. Diamond reports it due any moment.

LEVITAN: Anybody know what's on the tape?

DIAMOND: Not really. I think it's just a lot of miscellaneous newsfilm . . . Hold on, I can see her coming in . . . She's early . . . that's her all right . . . the wheels are now touching . . .

It is 3:23:30 pm, barely 11 hours since Harker started talking into

The first steps: the Chancellor and the President

"I wish to thank you for coming to visit us"

West German Honor Guard

his lip microphone at London Airport. As the jet touches the runway, Frank FitzPatrick, a CBS News traffic supervisor dashes out of the mobile unit, races to the plane, receives the tapes from a flight officer, rushes them through Customs, and brings them to the mobile unit where they are placed on the tape machine. At Studio 44, Levitan has alerted the Video Tape Room to be ready to start recording momentarily.

At 3:37 pm Diamond on the intercom informs Levitan that the tape is on the machine.

The first greeting

LEVITAN: *(to Video Tape Room)* Roll it!

On the three monitors above his head the first pictures of Harker, his hair ruffled by the wind, materialize on the screen. One critical element of the blueprint takes on actuality.

Meanwhile the major reality has already been under way in West Germany for the past four hours, ever since the President arrived to a tumultuous reception at Wahn Airport outside Bonn. Collingwood and Pierpoint had arrived an hour earlier in the Press plane. They were met by Leiser, Hewitt and Paskman who had been setting up facilities with the West German Television officials for the past 48 hours. Hewitt had been on the phone to London Airport almost continuously, making sure that everything was ready and working—the cables, the microwave relays, the converter, the video tape recorder.

When the wheels of the Boeing 707 jet carrying the President and his party touched the runway at 6:30 pm (Bonn time) the West German Television cameras swung into action, and with them Collingwood, Leiser, Pierpoint and Hewitt. In the bright afternoon sun Leiser gripped his microphone firmly and reported:

LEISER: Here comes Mr. Eisenhower. Stepping off the plane to applause, the first United States President to pay a friendly visit to Germany in history. Being greeted by Chancellor Adenauer, looking brown from his own holiday in Italy, greeting the rest of the West German government ... the former German Ambassador in Washington, now General Heusinger, head of the West German Armed Forces. Chancellor Adenauer is guiding the President to introduce him to the other members of the government. He just shook hands with the United States Ambassador, Mr. David Bruce. The President looks fit after his trip, which

"Looks fit after his trip"

Anthem follows anthem

The old refrain

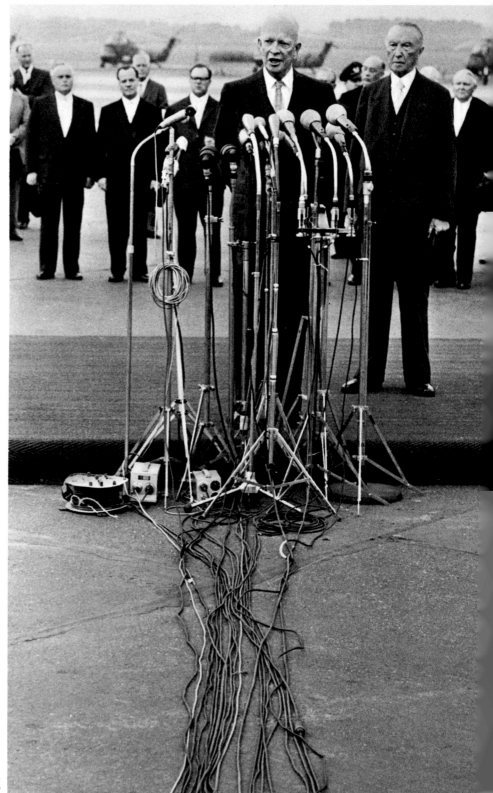

*"The American people
stand by your side"*

on a jet plane is not a long trip, from the United States. Walking with the Chancellor. Now the strains of the German National Anthem . . . the "Deutschlandlied." The familiar ring of older times, less happy times including those of the Nazis . . . but now the words are different, no longer "Germany, Germany, over all else." Accompanying Mr. Eisenhower and Dr. Adenauer is General Heusinger . . . and now the President . . . is trooping the line, trying to inspect an honor battalion of the West German Bundeswehr, a company each of soldiers, airmen and sailors.

West Germany's "White Mice" motorcycle police

Leiser translates Dr. Adenauer's welcoming address in which the Chancellor expresses his thanks to President Eisenhower for his visit to Western Germany and declares his confidence in the effectiveness of the visit to further the cause of peace and security in the world. It is immediately followed by President Eisenhower's greeting:

EISENHOWER: In my country the name Adenauer has come to symbolize the determination of the German people to remain strong and free. In the implementation of that determination the American people stand by your side and they send through me to you, the German people, their very best wishes for your successful efforts in this matter. And the American people stand by your side in insuring that the loyal free people of free Berlin will like yourselves continue always to enjoy that great privilege.

With the speed of light the pictures flow out of the cameras by cable and microwave to the Granada converter and video tape recorder 349 miles away at London Airport where BOAC Flight 683 stands by to receive the tapes the minute they are off the machine. The process continues virtually without interruption for the next hour-and-a-half (with a second plane standing by to pick up later portions of the broadcast) until the President and Chancellor Adenauer bid each other goodnight at the doors of the American Embassy in Bad Godesberg across the Rhine from Bonn.

At 6:05 am (New York time) August 27, Flight 683 arrives 35 minutes ahead of schedule at Idlewild with the tapes. The first pictures are on the air at 7 o'clock and are repeated at 7:20 and 7:40. Some 10 million people living within line of sight of the network's flagship station in New York, WCBS-TV, are the first Americans able to see an extended view (7 minutes, 57 seconds) of what took place in Bonn. The blueprint is working.

Reception in Bonn

Eager salute . . .

. . . happy response

12

At 8 am the pictures go out to audiences as far west as Ohio on the network's first news program of the day—*Richard C. Hottelet with the News* (If you were a farmer near Steubenville you could have seen them). They continue to be broadcast on the network throughout the day—at 9 am, at 1 pm on *Walter Cronkite with the News* and at 6:45 and 7:15 pm on *Douglas Edwards with the News*. As the day progresses more of the ceremonies and events in Bonn become visible in America with the arrival of planes carrying later tapes of the news coverage.

Producers Levitan and John Sharnik and Director Bill Greif spend the afternoon in the Video Tape Room viewing, editing and building the incoming tapes and films into a single vivid consecutive report of the President's experiences in Germany, with *live* up-to-the-minute news interpolations by Walter Cronkite in New York (e.g. the arrival of President Eisenhower later that day in England).

At 7:30 pm practically any television viewer in the country who had not seen one of the earlier broadcasts (as well as those who had) could watch a half-hour report of the entire proceedings that took place in Germany. (This was the first of 11 special broadcasts on the Eisenhower-Khrushchev journeys entitled *Eyewitness to History* and sponsored by The Firestone Tire and Rubber Company.)

Viewers followed the motorcade on its 20-mile drive from the Wahn Airport through the villages of the Rhine Valley into Bonn itself, the roadside lined with some 315,000 cheering West Germans. They saw the President and Dr. Adenauer enter the Palais Schaumburg, the German Chancellery, and heard CBS News correspondent Leiser describe the scene . . .

LEISER: The doors of the Chancellery opening in expectation that Chancellor Konrad Adenauer will come out and pose for the cameras with President Eisenhower. Chancellor Adenauer met the President at the airport last evening . . . This, of course, is the most important visit of state that has been paid to West Germany in the ten years that it has existed. The West Germans are enormously flattered at having been elevated to membership in a Western "Big Four" by the President's decision to visit Bonn as well as Paris and London. The crowd is still outside, still waving flags now for the television camera, again that "Help Us

"Der Alte"

"...to help melt the ice"

Interior, Foreign Ministry, Bonn

The whole country behind him:
Press Conference

Please," "Welcome Ike" from people of Berlin. And now the security police, the West German Border Police, that is, are trying to rope off the cameramen practically up to the Palais Schaumburg, and the honor guard itself is being dismissed and marches out. Here they come—out onto the porch of the Palais Schaumburg, President Eisenhower looking ruddy and rested.

Between them is Heinz Baber, their official interpreter who will be with them all day during their discussions, discussions that will be conducted in part with just a few men.

Wall map of the world

President Eisenhower unexpectedly interrupted his meeting at the Chancellery to call a press conference. Standing in front of a huge green world map covering an entire wall, the President responded to the questions of the hundred-odd European and American reporters present.

It was at this conference that the President disclosed the primary objective of his visit to Western Europe—namely, to help melt some of the ice in the "cold war." He pointed out that his forthcoming conversations with Premier Khrushchev were to "explore his mind to see whether any kind of proposal or suggestion that he can make, that would indeed make him a real leader in the search for peace in the world."

As the network's summary continues, viewers hear Collingwood analyze the significance of the West German phase of the President's visit:

Three Presidents:
Lubke,
Eisenhower,
Heuss

COLLINGWOOD: Here in Bonn, even more than in Paris, the President is finding the clearest and best reason for opposition to the course of personal diplomacy which he has undertaken. Chancellor Adenauer quite simply feels that any effort to reach an accommodation with the Russians today can only weaken, erode and blur the edges of the allied policy which the late Secretary of State Dulles maintained and that in that event Germany would be the first to suffer. The President has been eloquent in private and in public that he views the situation differently, that to him the international situation is so dangerous and so unstable that something must be done to try to solve that, that something must be done to try to find some avenue of peace. He will doubtless make that argument to Chancellor Adenauer as he will later to General de Gaulle. When he gets to England he won't have to make it because the British already agree with him.

Cronkite closes the program with a final bulletin:

CRONKITE: Well, tonight the President is in Britain for the second round of talks on this current trip. Half a million Londoners turned out to outdo the German welcome. Police called it the greatest such crowd in memory. Tomorrow the President visits the Queen at Balmoral and then goes into two days of talks with British leaders. For these events, the second part of the President's historic mission, our cameras and correspondents will again be on the scene . . .

Leiser monitors Collingwood, Wahn Airport

CBS News cameraman Schwartzkopff

Signalling directions, CBS News booth

A cable from Paskman provides some colorful background:

TELEVISION OPERATIONS ABROAD SIMILAR IN MANY RESPECTS TO AMERICAN OPERATIONS WITH NOMENCLATURE ONE BIG DIFFERENCE EXAMPLE GERMAN REMOTE UNIT CALLED AN UEBERTRAGUNGSWAGEN AND BRITISH CALL A REMOTE PICKUP AN OB MEANING OUTSIDE BROADCAST STOP THURSDAY MORNING HEWITT BEING ADDRESSED AS HERR DIREKTOR BY GERMAN TELEVISION CREWS AS HE SUPERVISED LIVE PICKUP EISENHOWER WHILE GRANADA BRITISH CREW THURSDAY AFTERNOON WAS ADDRESSING HIM AS QUOTE OLDBOY QUOTE AS HEWITT CALLED SHOTS ON IKE'S LONDON ARRIVAL STOP FAMILIAR ALERTING CUE "STAND BY" IS "ACHTUNG" IN GERMANY AND "WE RATHER READY CHAPS" IN BRITAIN AND "ATTENTION!" IN PARIS CBS NEWS INITIATIVE CONTRIBUTED TO EXPANDED COVERAGE BY EUROPEAN TELEVISION STOP EXAMPLE WEST GERMANS HAD NOT PLANNED LIVE COVERAGE IKE'S RIDE THROUGH BONN TO PALAIS SCHAUMBURG THURSDAY MORNING STOP THEY PROVIDED FACILITIES FOR US TO FEED LONDON FOR TAPING BUT STORY GOT SO GOOD THEY PICKED IT UP AFTER WE WERE ALREADY ON AIR STOP RESULT WAS THAT FOR SEVERAL MINUTES WEST GERMAN TELEVISION AUDIENCE WAS GETTING CBS NEWS CORRESPONDENT ERNEST LEISER'S DESCRIPTION IN ENGLISH WHICH HAD TO BE TRANSLATED INTO GERMAN UNTIL THEIR OWN COMMENTATOR CAME UP STOP GERMAN TELEVISION CREW UNSPOKE ENGLISH AND HEWITT HAD TO USE HAND SIGNALS TO CALL SHOTS.

A cable from Kendrick reports that he has just shipped a BBC video tape (running time 23 minutes) covering the President's arrival at London Airport. He itemizes its contents:

PLANE IN SIGHT, TOUCHDOWN, MACMILLAN WAITING, PLANE STOPPING, IKE ON BOARD, GREETING MACMILLAN, INSPECTION GUARD OF HONOR, MACMILLAN WELCOME, IKE'S REPLY, MOTORCADE STARTING, IKE WAVING TO CROWDS.

The tapes arrive on time—5:59 am Friday morning — and a motorcycle courier conveys them to the Video Tape Room. An hour later the pictures are on the air locally in New York, as with the German broadcast the day before, and at 8 am they go out over the network, where viewers see 4½ minutes of the President's first hours in England:

Arrival, London Airport

Speaker's stand, London Airport

Her Majesty's troops

Welcome Committee: Lord Gosford,
Herter, Macmillan, Lloyd

KENDRICK: A large crowd has gathered at London Airport North where VIPs normally arrive. Now this is a special car ... The Prime Minister managed to acquire this car from a private friend because the British Government has no official car of this type with an open body and the Prime Minister most earnestly wanted the fourteen-mile drive to the city of London to be in an open car so that tens of thousands of Britons could see the President whom they regard not only as the head of ... the leader of the Western Alliance but also as a warm personal friend and, of course, a freeman of the city of London and even a tenant of a castle in Scotland ... There have been many VIPs passing through London Airport but this is the one the British people seem to think most of and so there they go into the great western roads to the American Ambassador's residence in Regent's Park to start a five-day program beginning with a visit to the Queen at Balmoral Castle and then a weekend of political talks with the Prime Minister at Chequers, the Prime Minister's residence in the country.

Two sisters at Balmoral

That afternoon at 2:30 pm another cable from Kendrick reports that more tapes are due in New York in the next two hours containing "the best pictures yet on Ike's trip"—his greeting by Queen Elizabeth and Princess Margaret at Balmoral Castle in Scotland. Kendrick emphasizes that they are exclusive BBC pictures and that the British Broadcasting Corporation would appreciate being credited on the air.

They arrive and are shown on the air, properly credited, on the Douglas Edwards news program (less than 13 hours after the actual event) with the voice of BBC correspondent Richard Dimbleby in the background:

DIMBLEBY: The setting for this arrival of the President's and, of course, accompanying him, Prince Philip, is just as informal and friendly as it could be. There's a mixture here of the public and of those who work on the Balmoral estate for the Queen. Those who stand over there behind the gray wall on the far side of the road are all members of the estates. There in the center with their deer stalkers you can see some of the royal gillies as we call them perhaps in the Southgate. They, we hope on this nice fresh morning are not suffering too much from the after effects of the gillies' ball which was held in the castle last night which the royal family attended. This is the first time that an American President has ever come to Scotland—therefore obviously the first time an American President has ever come to Balmoral and for a Sassenach like myself from the other side of the border—Oh, here is Her Majesty the Queen. *(applause)* This is entirely unexpected. Now a private car drove down to the gate and out steps Her Majesty the Queen and Princess Margaret and that has really delighted and amazed the crowd around us down here on the roadside because we were all quite sure that the Queen was not going to come here and so she gets the welcome that she much deserves. Her Majesty, in a suit, we hope a warm one, it's a very cold

Inspecting the Queen's Own Royal Highland Fusiliers

Family visit

Trout reports from London

morning—her suit of pale blue, Princess Margaret in gray, at her side and she, no doubt, has been told that the procession is not very far away. Here she stands to greet her guest, to pay him a great distinction, not an unusual distinction, because, after all, in her own private house might she not have waited for him at her own front door... And here the procession of cars. Unusual to see the American flag, flying high on a royal car, the Queen's own car, with no number plates, flying the American flag. *(applause)* Her Majesty walks forward with Princess Margaret... Here're the cheers of the crowd. *(applause)*...The Guard of Honor... presents arms. *(bagpipes)* That short Royal Salute of the pipes, the salute pipes of war. With that, the Guard Commander comes forward, Captain Craigie Halkett, and presents the Guard for inspection by the President... As you may have heard, it's the First Battalion of the Royal Highland Fusiliers . . . As a soldier himself, inspection is a job that he finds easy to do.

Quips from a Queen

While the President is spending the first day of his weekend at Chequers with Prime Minister Macmillan, Kendrick in London manages to buttonhole Malcolm Muggeridge, the stormy petrel of British journalism and former editor of *Punch*, and becomes involved in a cantankerous interview. The next day—Sunday—millions of Americans get the taste of the famous Muggeridge wit as the interview is broadcast over the network.

Applause from a people

KENDRICK: There is no more astute and frequently caustic critic of the British scene than Malcolm Muggeridge. Malcolm, were you in the crowd that greeted the President?

MUGGERIDGE: No, Alex. I looked at it on television.

KENDRICK: In other words you did not get your feet stepped on.

MUGGERIDGE: No. But I saw it all.

KENDRICK: What do you suppose brought this tremendous mass of people out? Do you think it was sheer curiosity or do you think it was a sense of participation in history or just hero worship?

MUGGERIDGE: Oh, I think it was a bit of all three, you know, because people will turn out for almost anybody. Cromwell said to Fairfax, when a big crowd turned out for him, "You know, they'd turn out just as happily to see us hanged," and, of course, this is true. A big crowd turned out for Bulganin and Khrushchev here but it was a silent crowd and there's no doubt whatever that this was an enthusiastic and cheering crowd. I think the sense of it being a momentous occasion in a vague way also impressed people. It was built up in that sense and, finally, I think that the President of the United States does represent in Western Europe such hopes as people have of avoiding war and of continuing to live in their own way.

KENDRICK: Well, do you think then it was not really for the President himself but simply for what he stands, why he is here?

"the most fantastic enthusiasm"

Mother of Parliaments

*Kendrick
questions Muggeridge*

MUGGERIDGE: Well, of course, he's held in affection. He's very good at this sort of thing. His very qualities of simplicity which perhaps make him not the most distinguished of Presidents make him very effective in this sort of role. But at the same time it was also because he's simple. I was thinking while I was watching him of President Wilson coming over here when I was very small. He was rather a lantern-jawed man in a top hat and he aroused the most fantastic enthusiasm all over Europe and this was the same thing: the idea of America—which I distinguish, I might say, from the practice of America—symbolizes for people the hope for the future and I think you see the same thing with Eisenhower.

KENDRICK: Yes, but how do you relate this in terms, really, of present Anglo-American relations? Isn't the cousinship really between the two countries something that doesn't apply elsewhere?

"It's been a homecoming for the President"

MUGGERIDGE: I always think we are like a married couple. We are bound to quarrel but we have to live together for better or worse. We sometimes commit adultery too, incidentally, but those are little peccadilloes that we don't pay much attention to. Perhaps when Mr. Macmillan went over to Moscow that was a little infidelity, but, anyway, basically, for better or worse, 'till death do us part, and I use death advisedly, this is the situation.

KENDRICK: But Malcolm, the same sort of crowd turned out for the President in Germany. Now, would you say it was on the same terms as . . .

MUGGERIDGE: No.

KENDRICK: Then what's the difference?

MUGGERIDGE: Well, I think the basic difference is that from the point of view of the Germans, living as they do on the very borders of the U.S.S.R., America evidently and obviously represents their hope of survival and in that sense they have this tremendous feeling. Also, they were immensely concerned, I think, to impress the President with their unanimity and their newly-found strength, whereas here it's a remoter thing. But basically, it's the same. You've got this terrific anti-Americanism in this country. But underneath it there's not the slightest doubt that subconsciously or consciously people know that their future depends on the United States.

Collingwood analyzes the significance of the President's first days in Great Britain.

COLLINGWOOD: The most significant aspect of President Eisenhower's visit to Britain is not really the talks on matters of substance that he's having with Prime Minister Macmillan, but the mood, the tone of the visit, the extraordinary reception he got, the warmth on both sides which shone through every step of his progress from London Airport. It's been a homecoming for the President and neither he nor his hosts have made any secret of his and their delight at his being here. It's a remarkable demonstration of the special quality of the Anglo-American relationship and this is a factor of considerable international importance today not only because of the cooperation between the two countries but because of the jealousy of it—in Bonn where he's been and in Paris where he's going. The suspicions

Press tent, London: briefing correspondents

Touring the grounds, Chequers

Official spokesmen: Hagerty and Hope

of the French and the Germans can hardly but be enhanced by the evident comradeship and relaxed friendliness of his stay here. It's going to be hard for them not to believe that the President and the Prime Minister have made some sort of private agreement on all the issues which are at stake on this visit.

The talks at Chequers when the picture-taking was out of the way have been notably relaxed but nonetheless important. They talked about Laos and the India-Chinese border. Apparently they don't think that the troubles there are Russia's way of putting pressure on Eisenhower in his talks with Khrushchev. The feeling seems to be that it's China's pressure, not Russia, and because of it Britain is said to be no longer urging that this is the time the United States should recognize Red China. Perhaps most important, the President and the Prime Minister are said to have agreed that they can't just stop with the Eisenhower-Khrushchev talks, that some real negotiations have got to follow.

A visit to St. Paul's

Paskman cables Johnson some of the problems encountered by CBS News in London:

AMONG FRUSTRATIONS WAS BRITISH REFUSAL TO PERMIT CAMERA TRUCK IN IKE'S MOTORCADE INTO LONDON FROM AIRPORT STOP DESPITE AMERICAN INSISTENCE THAT SUCH FACILITIES ALWAYS PROVIDED AMERICAN CAMERAMEN IN UNITED STATES ON SUCH OCCASIONS THOSE THINGS JUST NOT DONE OVER HERE THEY EXPLAINED STOP WHILE SETTING UP FOR LIVE COVERAGE TRAFALGAR SQUARE OF IKE'S TRIP TO ST PAUL'S HAD TO CRAWL AROUND CATACOMBLIKE BASEMENT OF BRITAIN'S NATIONAL GALLERY TO FIND POWER OUTLET STOP PRESENCE OF BRITISH BOBBYS WITH FLASHLIGHTS "TORCHES" PROBING TOMBLIKE CELLAR REMINDFUL OF LAST ACT TYPICAL LATE SHOW THRILLER WHEN SCOTLAND YARD CLOSING IN ON JACK RIPPER STOP POLICE FIRST REFUSED PERMISSION SET UP LIVE CAMERAS TRAFALGAR SQUARE THEN POLICE INSPECTOR DECIDED PERSONALLY INVESTIGATE AND ENDED UP ENTHUSIASTICALLY SUGGESTING CAMERA LOCATIONS AND SHOTS EVERYBODY WANTS BE DIRECTOR STOP ENTIRE OPERATION WHICH DESPITE MUCH ADVANCE PLANNING POSSIBLE CAN BE SUMMED UP IN BRITISH TRAFFIC SIGN AMERICAN SIGNS SAY DANGEROUS CURVES BRITISH SAY DECEPTIVE BENDS STOP

The newspapermen were not without their problems, too. Some 300 American and British correspondents were summoned to a Press Conference on Sunday at which White House Press Secretary James Hagerty and Foreign Office spokesman Peter Hope briefed them on the President's conversation with Prime Minister Macmillan at Chequers.

Working things out: Hagerty, Paskman

A policeman's lot

The briefing quickly became acrimonious when Hope told the correspondents what the President and Prime Minister had for dinner (grouse). It drew an angry protest from an unidentified British correspondent who bitterly complained to Hagerty about the triviality of the information, saying "Are we to hear about international issues, or just what they ate?" Hagerty replied that he expected the President and the Prime Minister to present a report of their conversations on television the following night. It could be argued that this answer, to a newspaperman, was tantamount to pouring salt in a wound.

On Monday night in London President Eisenhower and Prime Minister Macmillan sat together informally at 10 Downing Street in front of a television camera and discussed world problems.

At 10 am Tuesday morning the CBS Television Network pre-empted its regularly scheduled program to present a special half-hour broadcast of the conversation. It nearly missed getting on the air. The BOAC jet with the tapes, due at Idlewild at 5:40 am, was four hours late, touching the runway twenty-two minutes before air time.

It was at this moment that the CBS News "dry-run" experiment of the week before proved its value. As the wheels of the jet touched the ground, CBS News Traffic Supervisor Frank FitzPatrick again sprinted from the remote mobile unit across the runway, a distance of approximately two football fields, obtained the tapes, and streaked back to the unit in time to start the transmission to Master Control at 9:56. As the red second-hand of the clock in Studio 44 hit the hour-mark, the first images were on the air.

On this broadcast perhaps more than on any previous one, television demonstrated its extraordinary power to reproduce and project the lights and shadows of human personality, revealing the personal characteristics of the two statesmen with striking clarity and definition. Each emerged on the screen as a veritable archetype of his nationality in feature, gesture and voice. There was no mistaking the Englishman any more than the American. It seemed as if they were typecast. They

Sprinter FitzPatrick

27

"Let's run over what we've said"

A point of interest

Television set-up, 10 Downing Street

spoke amiably and colloquially:

MACMILLAN: Let us run over what we've said tonight. I think it's of some importance. Our own relations between the two countries are probably as close, closer than they've ever been. That's something. We've got our NATO allies. There are difficulties, of course. Don't let's pretend that they don't exist. People take different points of view. There wouldn't be free governments if there weren't. And you have to, we have to, try and keep it all together.

We've got this problem of the under-developed countries which we really must work on, and we, I think, are ready to do our part. We've got a stronger economy at home, so we're able to give more abroad. And then, as you've said, you've got these contacts, these ideas developing, movements between the countries which will make the background, and that will help the statesmen to do what the peoples really want.

I think about it and I expect you do. And I think sometimes it's extraordinary. You and I sit in our rather lonely position sometimes and think what is it the people want and can we give it to them, and at the same time keep the principles we stand by. And I call it peace and justice, and those are the two words.

EISENHOWER: You know, one Frenchman gave a definition of freedom I like. He said freedom and liberty are merely the opportunity for self-discipline. Now we know that there are certain things that great nations can do if they are organized, harnessed as one, and go ahead and do it.

In the dictatorships this is all done by the order and by the police that make the order effective, so there is a continuity of policy and a unity of effort that is quite remarkable sometimes in Western eyes. But let's remember this. Our great strength is our dedication to freedom, and if we are sufficiently dedicated we will discipline ourselves so we'll make the sacrifices and do the things that need to be done. And that is exactly what you and I, I think, are trying to teach ourselves, our friends, our own peoples, and, hopefully, Mr. Khrushchev.

MACMILLAN: Well, Mr. President, I think our time is rather drawing to an end. We mustn't go on too long. We've got some guests waiting. But I would like to say again how very glad—I know I speak on behalf of every single man, woman and child in this country, of whatever party, or creed, or anything—how glad we are to have you with us.

It isn't only for what you represent, the great country you represent. Of course it's that. But it's because we've known you all these years and it's for what you are yourself. We've always known you from the seventeen years ago when you took command of our great forces and carried them through to victory. And we welcome you here. Now we've got our guests, and among our guests, I am happy to say, we have Sir Winston Churchill.

EISENHOWER: Well, I must say you embarrass me. But I'm delighted Sir Winston's going to be here. And now do you mind me saying just one word directly to your people? I want to thank everybody that's had a part in showing his kindness and British hospitality to me and to my party. And in doing so, to show also that respect for the principles on which both our countries are founded and established

Second thoughts

29

An exclusive interview: Foot, Kendrick, Boothby

Television instructions

"How did it strike you?"

and maintained, that we in our country so revere. So finally, may I say this one word. God save your gracious Queen and all her people.

The conversation was immediately discussed in an exclusive television interview arranged by Kendrick with Lord Robert Boothby, member of the House of Lords, and Michael Foot, a former Labor M.P., now editor of the British weekly *Tribune*. It was hammer and tongs right from the start:

KENDRICK: We have been sitting and viewing together with fifteen or perhaps twenty million other people in this country, the television appearance of the Prime Minister and President tonight. And since both you gentlemen are politicians, as well as being journalists, how did it strike you?

BOOTHBY: Well, I wasn't expecting very much, to be frank, and therefore I thought that it was a remarkable performance. A very skillful performance on both their parts. I think the three things that came through to me were first of all the vast improvement in Anglo-American relations. It was clear that those two men were on very cordial terms and I couldn't help thinking back to Suez and thinking that we've made a great advance since then, which was nothing but a good thing. The second thing is that I think the President came nearer to accepting a summit conference than he has hitherto done—and I think that's a good thing. And I was finally delighted with the emphasis they both put upon the necessity for giving massive assistance to the under-developed countries. One thing disappointed me and that is that they never mentioned disarmament, which I think is probably the most important aspect of the lot.

FOOT: Well, I'm sorry to introduce something of a jarring note into this discussion and I'm certainly very glad that not only on this occasion but that President Eisenhower is being given a proper and hospitable reception in this country. That's only right and proper. But when you look at the method of putting things across on this program, I think it reduces international relations to something like the level of farce, because here, after all, there are a lot of top problems to be settled in the world—not only between this country and the United States, but between the Western world and the Eastern world. And we have all these problems pushed aside and smothered in a kind of sentimental slush, because that is really what it amounts to. I don't think it's good to encourage people to think these are the real problems. I don't think it's going to assist. I think it merely blurs the issue—and so far from having issues blurred, what we want to do to solve them is to have them clear.

BOOTHBY: Well, it made me feel rather good, Michael, you know. You may argue that it was a great mistake that they should have appeared on television at all. I'm not by any means convinced about that.

I think it will have brought a feeling of reassurance and hope to very many millions of people. You couldn't expect them to get down to the hard tacks of the business, to deal with hard stuff, the concrete problems which we know divide us, not only from the Russians but amongst ourselves . . .

Video tape unit, London

Hewitt at Trafalgar Square

Collingwood on the Embankment

Wartime comrades:
Churchill and Montgomery

FOOT: Well, we knew in advance they weren't going to scratch each other's eyes out and I don't want them to scratch each other's eyes out. I want them to talk about the real problems that face the world.

If they're not prepared to talk about them, well, don't put on a great program which is supposed to be the President of the United States and the Prime Minister of Britain talking about things that matter.

The two Englishmen continued to go after each other relentlessly until their air time expired.

The program was barely off the air before Johnson in New York dashed off a cable to Kendrick explaining the narrow margin of time in which the network was able to broadcast the event.

"Skin of teeth" operation

IN REAL HAIRY SKIN OF YOUR TEETH OPERATION WE MADE TEN AM NEW YORK BROADCAST TIME TODAY OF IKE MAC TELEVISION TALK STOP PLANE TOUCHED END OF RUNWAY TWENTY TWO MINUTES BEFORE AIR TIME AND VIDEO TAPE REEL INSIDE OUR MOBILE UNIT READY TO ROLL FROM TOP UNSEEN AND UNEDITED AT FOUR MINUTES BEFORE AIR TIME WHILE DIAMOND AT AIRPORT RACKING UP SECOND REEL WITH SLAMBANG DOGFIGHT BETWEEN FOOT AND BOOTHBY STOP EXCELLENT TELEVISION AND SO GOOD THAT WCBSTV ASKED RERUN TONIGHT AND FINALLY NETWORK DECIDED RERUN EIGHT TO EIGHT THIRTY PM STOP DIAMOND STOLLMACK AND OTHERS GAVE TOPNOTCH UNDER PRESSURE PERFORMANCE HERE STOP NBC FILM ON SAME PLANE AND THEIR SHOW ON IKE MAC TELEVISION CHAT WON'T BE SEEN UNTIL AFTER OUR REPEAT TONIGHT STOP MANY THANKS ALL HANDS AND LONDON PLEASE CONVEY OUR CONGRATULATIONS GRANADA PARTICULARLY FOR FINE VIDEO TAPING AND CONVERTING WORK FROM BONN ON REGARDS.

Following his television conversation with the Prime Minister the President returned to the American Embassy. He spent the next day (Tuesday) virtually free of official engagements. That night he gave a private dinner for some of his wartime associates. Among them were Sir Winston Churchill and Field Marshals Montgomery and Alexander. On Wednesday he flew to Paris.

Hewitt and Paskman have preceded him by 24 hours. For some time prior to their arrival Arthur Schoenfuss, in charge of European technical operations for the CBS Television Network, together with CBS

Arrival, Le Bourget

Shoulder to shoulder

Friendly gesture

The sweep of history

News correspondent Lou Cioffi, had been negotiating with French television and Eurovision authorities to set up the necessary facilities for coverage—particularly with regard to making video tape recordings of the President's motorcade down the Champs Élysées. After a certain amount of resistance, the officials reluctantly agreed to allocate certain camera positions. Unhappy with the allocations, Hewitt, in his best fractured French, attempted to persuade the Eurovision technicians to move the cameras to obtain more favorable angles. It was heavy going in every sense of the term. When the final camera had been shifted an exasperated French technician turned to CBS News Paris chief David Schoenbrun, saying, "Okay. But if Hewitt wants us to move the Arch of Triumph two feet to suit his picture angles, let me tell you, *mon ami*, the answer is *Non!*"

Most Americans on Thursday night who watched the events in Paris on their television screens had reason to be grateful for Hewitt's doggedness. It was a spectacular sight as picked up by television cameras and described by Schoenbrun:

SCHOENBRUN: This is Paris, the capital of France and capital of NATO—the last, but in a political sense, perhaps the most important capital, certainly the most critical of the capitals visited. President Eisenhower didn't have any grave or intense problems to face in Germany or in England. But here in France there are deep-seated grievances, genuine conflicts of policy on such vital issues as Algeria, the functioning of the Atlantic alliance and atomic testing. These are real differences of policy between the governments despite the continuing friendship between the peoples of France and of America. Everybody's been saying for many months now that these differences could not be resolved, that true unity of purpose and full spirit of the alliance could not be restored until the two wartime comrades and peacetime Presidents got together. And now they are together again here in Paris. President Eisenhower and President de Gaulle last rode up on the Champs Élysées together when both of them were generals in 1945, in the month of June when President de Gaulle gave General Eisenhower, his wartime comrade, one of the highest decorations available to him, the Cross of Liberation, and he's ever since been known as "the liberator" of the French people. *(crowd cheers)* They're moving into vision now at the Arch of Triumph at what is called the Place de l'Étoile, the star-shaped square. *(band plays—crowd cheers)* Now the sword and the torch which rekindles the flame, a symbolic gesture to keep the torch of liberty flying and glowing in Paris. *(crowd cheers)* The salute to the dead . . .

Maison du Rhum (advt.)

"The answer is NON!"

"Long Live the President of the United States!"

"I have one small French phrase"

In perfect formation

Schoenbrun reports that earlier in the day the two heads of states discussed the "tragic" and "most important" problem of Algeria, emphasizing that what de Gaulle needs above all else is the support of the United States. Viewers follow the motorcade as it passes the Hotel de Ville and turns into the Town Hall Square.

SCHOENBRUN: More than a hundred thousand people have been gathered in the Square and perhaps as many as a quarter of a million all around this huge square waiting for hours to see the two chiefs of state of the French and American Republics. *(cheers—trumpets)* Now from the steps of Town Hall the President of the French Republic. *(cheers)*

DE GAULLE: *(Schoenbrun translating)* I have personally a profound joy to find in him again the good, the dear, the loyal companion at whose side I walked along the path of very difficult times, in the books of history. I can tell you, and I say it here today, that between him and me, everything always worked well. *(crowd cheers)* Long live General Eisenhower! Long live the President of the United States! Long live the United States of America! *(crowd cheers)* Long live America, the eternal friend of France! *(crowd cheers)*

Now the President replies:

EISENHOWER: President de Gaulle, President of the Municipal Council, Parisians, and citizens of France. *(crowd cheers)* When the heart is full, the tongue is very likely to stumble. Should I try to express to you today the true feelings, the true sentiments that now inspire me, I should be completely unable to speak at all.

I can say only that over the years this city, this country, has become like it has for almost every American, something that is very dear, very real and truly a part of the kind of world in which we want to live. We have been allies for many years. From the days of Lafayette, back in the late Seventeen-hundreds, to this very moment, America cherishes the friendship, the loyal support, the loyal cooperative efforts that have always been hers whenever she needed them from France. *(crowd cheers)*

To become more personal let me speak for a moment about your great President, General de Gaulle. I met him in London more than seventeen years ago. Our acquaintanceship and friendship grew and developed in Algiers and again when we were in Britain. And then I met him again in France as he began the process of reconstruction in this great country. And since that time I have kept in touch with him. Now it is my great privilege to work with him again in the great purposes that he has just explained. Those of finding a path to the peace and the security for all the world *(crowd cheers)* so that you, your children, your grandchildren, like all those in other parts of the world, in all the continents, can live in confidence, can develop in themselves all their God-given qualities and become truly people without fear. People that love liberty will never let it slip away from them either by neglect or under threat, and will march down the road to the future with all of the faith in their God and in themselves that will make

A reflected view

Reception, Élysée Palace

37

Overlooking the Place d'Étoile

An elderly assessment

Five miles per hour

City of Light

everybody, all of us, a happy people. *(crowd cheers)* And so all I can say again, to this throng, to all the people who lined the Champs Élysées, who were along the streets and the boulevards as we came down here—I have one small French phrase that I think expresses my feelings:"Je vous aime tous." *(crowd cheers)*

Having learned that the President while in Paris would also talk with representatives of other European nations, notably the Italian Prime Minister, Johnson had cabled Winston Burdett, CBS News Rome correspondent, to cover this aspect of the proceedings. Burdett appears on the screen reporting the points of view of Italy, Belgium and Holland.

Burdett on Italy

BURDETT: The smaller nations have feared above all that an American-French quarrel would force them to choose between the United States and a European community led by France. They are willing to appease the French, to mollify the French, to flatter the French. They agree that France must play a leading role in the European community. But they are unwilling to follow France or to permit de Gaulle to boost French influence in Western Europe as a counterforce, a counterattraction and as a bargaining or blackmailing weapon against the United States. For all of these countries and for West Germany as well, the United States is essential to their security and there is no substitute for American leadership in Europe. On the one hand they fear that America may be driven away by de Gaulle's intransigence, and on the other, afraid that de Gaulle and France may be driven into angry isolation. In short, they fear that NATO itself might be wrecked by a transatlantic fall. The statesmen who saw President Eisenhower today were anxious to make clear that de Gaulle does not and cannot speak for them or for Europe. They hope that President Eisenhower in turn has been able to make this clear to de Gaulle and for the sake of the Western Alliance has been able to do this without offending this sensitive and stubborn man.

Burdett is followed by Collingwood who compares the present occasion with the previous receptions in West Germany and England:

COLLINGWOOD: It is just as friendly here, but it has not been easy as it was in Bonn and in London. For General de Gaulle has a list of grievances to present to the President which, in themselves, would have justified a meeting between the two men if the Khrushchev-Eisenhower talks had never been arranged. Here in Paris, inevitably, the Eisenhower-Khrushchev exchanges have been subordinated to the opportunity for these two old wartime associates to meet again and for General de Gaulle to present to President Eisenhower his bill of complaints. There's nothing new about this bill of complaints. President Eisenhower has known about them for a long time. General de Gaulle time and again, at long distance, has made it clear that France wants an equal partnership with the United States and Britain in the planning and solution of world-wide political and military problems. He's made no secret of the fact that France wants American support for her policy toward Algeria, whatever that policy may be, and that she wants American help in developing her atomic weapons . . .

Monitor, CBS News Paris Bureau

"More than one hundred thousand"

The French television image

Actually there's not a great deal that the President can specifically do to accommodate the General. That is, he can't singlehandedly change the laws which Congress has made about the sharing of atomic secrets. Nor can he, by himself and on the spur of the moment, commit the United States to the support of France's policy in Algeria, even if the General has revealed that policy to him in detail, as he is said to have done.

General de Gaulle knows these things. But there are things which the President can do to convince the General and to convince France that the United States has France's interests in heart . . . And that after all is what General de Gaulle really wants and what the people of France want . . . That seems to be the real explanation for this third tremendous, dramatic welcome that President Eisenhower received on his visit to Europe.

Signs on a Paris subway

From New York Cronkite winds up the program:

CRONKITE: The President has now completed the business of his trip to Europe. Act One, so to speak, of his dramatic excursion into personal diplomacy. In the 12 days left before his meetings with Khrushchev, the next act in the drama, the President plans a holiday weekend in Scotland and then he flies back to Washington to clear his desk of accumulated domestic matters before his talks with the Russian leader which begin a week from next Tuesday. We'll have a full report on the results of the President's European tour and how they might affect the talks with Khrushchev from the CBS News team which covered the Presidential tour . . . next Sunday at this same time in "Prelude to Khrushchev."

"General de Gaulle knows these things"

Several days earlier the contingent of CBS News correspondents had been alerted by cable to prepare this "full report" wrapping up the significance of the President's travels in Europe. The request was explicit. The report was to take the form of a 14-minute panel discussion Friday morning in Paris which would consist of answering a series of salient questions prepared by CBS News in New York. These questions were designed to elicit the kind of answers many Americans were eager to have concerning the President's trip. The cable spelled out the questions.

The correspondents were instructed to fly to New York at the conclusion of their discussion in order to be available at the television studio in the event that further editing became necessary, or to interpolate the significance of any last-minute news breaks. Finally, they were asked to attend a special meeting on Saturday morning with Sig Mickelson, President of CBS News, and Assistant CBS News Director Johnson in the latter's office in the Grand Central Building.

Still sleepy-eyed and unshaven from their overnight flight from Paris,

French "security" fireman

Hewitt, Collingwood, Schoenbrun, Cioffi

Les Spahis:
Algerian Guard of Honor

London and Bonn—Collingwood, Schoenbrun, Kendrick and Leiser, together with CBS News' peripatetic producer-director Hewitt, gather in Johnson's office Saturday morning at 10:30. It is a unique situation. Four correspondents who on the previous afternoon had made a video tape recording in Paris of their analysis of the President's European trip, now sit watching themselves, the following morning, on a television monitor in New York. A case of the eyewitnesses eyewitnessing the eyewitnesses. Monitoring the tape with them are Cronkite, Sharnik and Greif who have the responsibility of putting the show on the air Sunday night. As the last frame fades from the monitor Mickelson expresses his enthusiasm and asks each of the correspondents whether they are willing to stand on what they said. All agree. Sharnik then explains that in putting the show together he intends to introduce the panel discussion with two-minute montages of each correspondent narrating a reprise of his personal experiences in Bonn, London and Paris. It meets with general approval and the meeting disbands.

At 7:30 Sunday night the program goes out over the network as planned on the fourth special half-hour broadcast of *Eyewitness to History*. As it enters its final minutes Collingwood asks a leading question:

COLLINGWOOD: Well, now let's get to what may really be the key question that we've been asked: How have the President's talks in Europe strengthened his position for the forthcoming talks with Khrushchev?

LEISER: Well, I think a very important thing, Charles, is that Eisenhower's reaction to Europe, Europe's reaction to Eisenhower, have strengthened the President's own self-confidence. He sees himself once again as the leader of the grand alliance, I'm sure.

KENDRICK: Well also, it must have given Khrushchev some idea that Ike was well received and the people of Europe had confidence in him and that they saw in him their old concept of a vigorous leader of the Western Alliance.

SCHOENBRUN: That's the key to the whole thing, this old idea of Eisenhower as a sick, inarticulate man who couldn't form his own policies . . .

KENDRICK: Which was deliberately built up in Europe.

SCHOENBRUN: That's right. That's gone. Khrushchev is dealing with a man that's alive, vigorous, thinking for himself, acting for himself, and speaking for the people of Europe.

Battle monument, Arch of Triumph

Paris hat fashions

Hotel de Ville, Paris City Hall

Camera bug, Paris style

*"They're moving into vision
at the Arch of Triumph"*

COLLINGWOOD: Well, with your permission, this is the line that I'll take in answering these questions, I've made some notes here. One, don't minimize the importance of the crowds which greeted President Eisenhower everywhere. They show among other things the immense popular support, at present, for what the President is trying to do in this new phase of his diplomacy. Two, I think we should say that in his talks he covered a great deal of ground in general, but didn't settle anything very specific. Three, there still remain differences among the Western nations, but the atmosphere once again, at present, has been immeasurably improved by his trip. Four, we all agree that for one reason or another a summit meeting is closer now. Five, the talks have strengthened the President in his position vis-a-vis Khrushchev when they meet, both psychologically in terms of the confidence in himself which he must have gained, and two, by demonstrating for Mr. Khrushchev and everyone else the fact that the whole West, both leaders and the people, trust his leadership in this new era of diplomacy.

Cronkite makes a final announcement:

CRONKITE: Next in this new era of face-to-face diplomacy: the confrontation that Premier Khrushchev has incessantly talked about and worked toward for the last two years or more. This will be a week from Tuesday, on September 15th, when Khrushchev meets the President in Washington. Without doubt one of the most dramatic single events of this postwar period. Once again our live television cameras will be on the scene, and we'll be back that evening at this same time with a full report of that event and its significance.

Over the weekend the President has been relaxing at the apartment in Culzean Castle in Scotland which the Scottish people had presented to him in gratitude for his wartime achievements. Although no important news was expected from this quarter, CBS News correspondent Robert Pierpoint and cameraman Tommy Craven stood by in the event that the President should decide to make a statement. As it turned out, they spent most of the time filming him on the golf course.

At 11 pm Sunday night the films are shown over the CBS Television Network with Walter Cronkite reporting.

CRONKITE: President Eisenhower went to this old church this morning in the heart of the Tam o' Shanter country celebrated by poet Bobbie Burns. And then the President made such a bee line for the golf course that he even skipped lunch and arrived at the course before his playing companions.

This was the President's last day at Culzean Castle. He announced today that he's cutting his visit short, apparently because of concern about the Laos situation and Congressional adjournment. He'll leave Scotland tomorrow morning, stop off for lunch in Iceland and arrive in Washington late in the afternoon. . . .

Yesterday, the President even went for a ride in a little pony cart with the Marquess and Marchioness of Ailsa and their children . . . Charles and Elizabeth.

On-the-scene broadcaster

"...a bee line for the golf course"

Par 71, score 83

Cronkite reports on Scotland

The jaunt began on the grounds of the Castle Culzean, but then led out onto public roads . . . and into view of scores of reporters and cameramen barred from the grounds. In fact, the crowds became so thick that the cart was turned around and headed back into seclusion.

The high point of every day the President has been at the Castle Culzean has been the round of golf at the nearby Turnberry course. Large crowds have turned out to see the President in action, and he's given them a good show . . . he's gotten off several tee shots with the spectators watching . . . apparently unconcerned by the audience . . . And his game has been fairly good on the exacting, par-71 course . . . shooting from 83 to 89.

Douglas Edwards with the news

The following night on the Douglas Edwards news program television viewers watched the President's arrival in Washington earlier that day and heard him say:

EISENHOWER: There was serious purpose to this visit. All of us — the heads of government in West Germany, Britain and France—we knew that we were united in basic principle and purpose and in our pursuit of peace.

But always there comes up among friends, who are necessarily separated at such distances, small details of procedures, and methods and tactics in the pursuit of great programs. These have to be talked out. Every serious—indeed, I don't want to use the word serious—every troublesome little problem of this type has been talked out, and I am quite certain that for the moment at least everything is going splendidly.

There is nothing else, there is no other single fact of the modern world that is now so important, I think, as this: that the people of the Western world have for each other a very deep, abiding affection, mutual trust—and in this there was a tremendous personal, moral and indeed a material and economic strength.

The first phase of CBS News coverage is finished. Its dimensions are indicated in a cable from Kendrick—the last of more than 200 that have passed between CBS News in New York and its correspondents, directors, technicians and engineers abroad during the President's travels. It read in part:

CBS COVERAGE IKE IN EUROPE WAS OPERATION OF UNPRECE-
DENTED SCALE INVOLVING FIRSTLY FULL USE OF EUROVISION
LINK WITH ITS COMBINATION OF TELEVISION SERVICES POST
OFFICES AND GOVERNMENTS ELEVEN EUROPEAN COUNTRIES STOP
SECONDLY FULL USE GRANADA TELEVISION LTD LIVE CAMERAS
VIDEO TAPE RECORDING AND CONVERSION FROM EUROPEAN TO
AMERICAN LINAGE STOP THIRDLY BBC LIVE REMOTES WHICH THEN
KINESCOPED ON FILM AS WELL VIDEO TAPED STOP FOURTHLY CBS
NEWS OWN FULL FILM COVERAGE FOR SYNDICATION AND ALL

Home again

"There was serious purpose to this visit"

The Vice President
shows the way

NEWS PROGRAMS STOP FIFTHLY FULL RADIO COVERAGE USING
REMOTE PICKUPS FOR LIVE BROADCASTS AND LONDON STUDIOS
OF BBC.

FOCAL POINT OF CBS EFFORT WAS MASSIVE GRANADA EFFORT
INVOLVING THREE HUGE VANS AND MOBILE ELECTRONIC CAMERA
UNIT BROUGHT DOWN FROM MANCHESTER 200 MILES AWAY STOP
THIS QUOTE SECRET WEAPON UNQUOTE QUIETLY INSTALLED
PANAMERICAN MAINTENANCE AT LONDON AIRPORT WHERE FOR
DURATION IKE'S STAY IT WORKED IN VERY SHADOW PRESIDENT'S
BIG ORANGE AND SILVER JET . . . ENTIRE TECHNICAL OPERATION
UNDER SUPERVISION GRANADA'S DIRECTOR ENGINEERING REG
HAMMANS WHO REFUSES ESTIMATE FOOTAGE OF VIDEO TAPE
USED IN CBS OPERATION BUT SAYS THAT JUST LIKE IKE'S JOURNEY
WOULD EXTEND FROM BONN TO LONDON AND BACK TO PARIS . . .

CBS News cameraman Craven

Kendrick's cable concludes: "Although this was the first time such
an operation was tried and despite near misses on intergovernmental
cable facilities and catching planes, the frustrations were really at a
minimum and by the time 'Operation Ike' ended, it had become a rou-
tine procedure with invaluable experience for the next time anything
like this is tried."

CLOSE-UP, U.S.A.

For television the task of covering Premier Khrushchev's visit to the United States presented a far simpler technical problem than the President's European journey. This time television would be operating on its home grounds, free from the hurdles of unfamiliar language, geography, and conflicting television standards. To be sure it would still involve the severe dislocation of program schedules, originating broadcasts from hundreds of remote points throughout the nation, and the complex logistics of moving men and equipment. But, essentially, this was standard operating procedure multiplied by a known, though formidable, factor.

On the other hand, the presence of an unknown factor created a problem of an entirely different order. This was the air of uncertainty surrounding the confrontation of the Soviet Premier with the American people—a meeting charged with the tensions of more than a dozen years of "cold war" and more recently inflamed by the issues of Berlin, Tibet and Laos. Nobody really knew what to expect on the occasion of this meeting either in terms of the reactions of the public or of the Premier.

A week before his arrival it became known that the Premier's presence in this country would be marked by the tightest security precautions ever taken for a foreign visitor.

He would be guarded by some 15,000 military men, police, detectives, national guardsmen, federal security agents and members of the Soviet secret police. In Washington arrangements had been made to batten down all manhole covers along the 15-mile motorcade route from Andrews Air Force Base to Blair House, where the Premier would spend his first night. Window shopping by the public would be prohibited and all strangers barred from buildings and rooftops along the procession route. Clearly none of this was calculated to make the job of news coverage any easier.

"Profile of Khrushchev"

Strawser paves the way

The Khrushchevs at home

In a 15-minute nationwide television report to the nation on September 10, President Eisenhower alluded to this aspect of the impending visit, then only five days off:

EISENHOWER: I have every confidence that our people will greet Mr. Khrushchev and his wife and family with traditional American courtesy and dignity. We cannot fail to accord him the same consideration which the Soviet people gave to Vice President and Mrs. Nixon.

The following night on the Douglas Edwards news program the CBS Television Network presented an advance view of the first scenes of Washington that Premier Khrushchev would see on his arrival. CBS News correspondent Neil Strawser supplied the commentary:

STRAWSER: Khrushchev's first ground view of the Capitol Building from South Capitol Street Bridge is combined with a view of industries along the river.

As his automobile moves off the bridge on up South Capitol Street *this* is the view on the left. . . A row of houses in the slum-blighted area of southwest Washington. And these are almost the only homes he will see on the drive, which follows a route untraveled by most visitors, because he's arriving at a different airport. The houses are soon to be torn down . . . but to Khrushchev . . . this may be proof of his already stated belief that most Americans live in poverty even here, almost in the shadow of the Capitol.

Turning into Independence Avenue he'll see the impressive Health Education and Welfare Building . . . but on the other side . . . rows on rows of so-called temporary government buildings with paint peeling from their now-aging walls. Here thousands of government employees also work. Things improve as the Premier drives on up past the Agricultural Department and joins the usual ceremonial route through a portion of downtown Washington. Finally, he drives past the White House where he'll dine Tuesday night with the President, to newly-painted Blair House, the President's Guest House, the arrival here ending the first rather dubious chapter in the education of a Soviet Premier.

On Sunday night at 6 pm the television audience learned more about the character and accomplishments of the visitor from a half-hour television broadcast entitled "Profile of Khrushchev" narrated by CBS News correspondent Howard K. Smith. It consisted of a sequence of Soviet films, still photographs, and animated sketches depicting the revolutionary youth of the Premier, his rise to power, and some of the basic changes he had introduced into Soviet society since the death of Stalin. Smith concluded his report with an analysis of public opinion regarding the impending visit.

Early comrades

Late comrades

Anti-Communist, Carnegie Hall demonstration

An antagonist

Sidewalk flare-up

SMITH: Mr. Khrushchev will find America—if the nation's capital is a measure of it—in a curious mood.

Most people think the trip is a good idea. The "cold war" has been stagnant so long, the monster weapons have grown so deadly, that something new must be tried to break the log-jam and ease tension.

It is distinctly a minority who oppose the visit and will wear black armbands and demonstrate in protest.

But even the majority who favor it admit to massive misgivings. There is a lingering fear that the visitor may get false impressions of weakness or complacency from what is, in fact, courtesy. He may interpret hospitality to mean enthusiasm for what he represents.

Our diplomatic leaders, oddly, are delighted at both moods. They are glad that most favor the visit, and equally satisfied that there is a restraint of doubt.

A newspaper has suggested the mood should be one of courteous skepticism. A senator has said we should, in meeting the guest, be civil but silent. In one form and another spokesmen have proposed a judicious combination of firmness and readiness to conciliate.

In that spirit we look forward to what will undoubtedly be about the most interesting two weeks in the "cold war."

CBS News' Smith, Niven, Bliss and Schorr

Earlier that day CBS News had sent a film cameraman to cover an anti-Khrushchev demonstration which flared up momentarily in New York when 500 members of The American Friends of the Anti-Bolshevik Bloc of Nations held a mass meeting and parade in Manhattan. The films were seen next morning at 7 am in New York.

On Monday morning, September 14, Americans awoke to the extraordinary fact that a Soviet rocket had hit the moon. Television's battalions of correspondents, cameramen, technicians, producers, directors and news editors were already deployed in and around Washington and Andrews Air Force Base in readiness for the Soviet Premier's arrival on the following morning. Weeks before, the three television networks had arranged with Mr. Hagerty and other White House information officials to "pool" their video and sound equipment and produce a common picture of the arrival. However, each network would provide its own commentary.

The specifics of CBS News' participation in this coverage had previously been spelled out in a 5-page single-spaced memorandum circulated throughout the organization by Ted Koop, Washington administrator for CBS News. Howard K. Smith, Paul Niven, former CBS News cor-

Downs gives the "high-up" view

Schorr recalls previous trips

"Sincere greeting to Premier Khrushchev . . ."

Camera scaffolding,
Andrews Air Force Base

respondent in Moscow, and Whitman Bassow, former UPI correspondent in Moscow, were assigned to cover the arrival at Andrews Air Force Base. Charles von Fremd with an off-the-air monitor was assigned to the corner lobby of the U.S. Department of Agriculture Building at 14th Street and Independence Avenue, the point at which the ceremonial parade was to start.

Speakers' platform with placecards

Bill Downs, veteran CBS News war correspondent, was posted in the Ladies' Lounge of the National Press Club Building for a "high-up" view of the parade. Daniel Schorr, who had also formerly been stationed in Moscow for CBS News, covered the proceedings from the roof of the Mills Building, and Robert Pierpoint, CBS News White House correspondent, was posted in front of the Executive Offices Building. Each man had a specific assignment . . . in the words of Koop's memorandum:

At anchor, in New York, will be Douglas Edwards. He will have an "eye on the parade" window and will open and close the special program and give the basic parade description from his anchor studio. From this studio, too, will come the necessary station breaks; the fills, as needed during the motorcade trip into Washington; the "please stand by" telop for video trouble, and another telop for use in the event of emergency along the Suitland Parkway where the pool can provide voice coverage only from the CBS News reporter in the pool NBC-TV mobile unit . . .

At the Department of Agriculture, von Fremd will give the only minute description of the marching units. His remarks, too, should point up similarities and differences with customary Washington parades.

Downs, in the Ladies' Lounge at the Press Club, can give detailed summaries of previous Khrushchev visits to other lands, a listing of distinguished Americans who have visited Russia . . .

Schorr at the Mills Building can give full range to his personal experiences in Moscow and other Iron Curtain capitals which Khrushchev has been visiting. Schorr should also brief himself on the interior of the President's Guest House to be able to describe it as Khrushchev enters.

At the White House, Pierpoint can wind up with a run-down of Eisenhower quotes, hopes and fears for the meetings.

This division of reportorial coverage is important if CBS News is to provide the news-in-depth and "mature" coverage expected of it.

At 10:47 o'clock Tuesday morning, September 15, some 13 minutes before the scheduled arrival at Andrews Air Force Base, CBS News broke into the regularly scheduled network program with a bulletin announcing that the plane carrying Premier Khrushchev and his party

Too big to reach the apron of the field

Waiting patiently

Edwards from the "anchor studio," New York

had been delayed by head winds over Boston. A second and third bulletin followed at intervals of approximately three-quarters-of-an-hour and a half-hour.

At 12:20 pm, millions of viewers, engrossed in one of their favorite daytime serial dramas on the CBS Television Network, watched a distraught father describe to a detective the circumstances of his daughter's disappearance, and heard him say, "She had blonde hair, blue eyes and drove a white foreign car." Suddenly their mood was shattered by an alien voice—that of Doug Edwards, appearing on the screen from CBS News' "anchor" studio in New York.

First steps on solid ground

EDWARDS: We interrupt this program for a CBS News special report, Douglas Edwards reporting. Soviet Premier Nikita Khrushchev has become the first ruler of Russia ever to set foot on American soil. His giant TU-114 turbo-prop plane was delayed by head winds on its flight from Boston on its way to Andrews Air Force Base in historic Maryland, 15 miles from the heart of Washington.

CBS News is standing by with 20 cameras to cover the opening chapter of this visit, the arrival and welcome by President Eisenhower and the motorcade to Blair House, newly named the President's Guest House, and Khrushchev's residence-to-be.

The story begins at Andrews Air Force Base where the guard and security men have been at their posts since early this morning, so let's go over there now with Howard K. Smith reporting.

A bouquet for the Premier

SMITH: This is Andrews Air Force Base . . . It is an extremely odd experience in this city, where there have been so many investigations, to be prepared to welcome amid pomp and ceremonies the world's foremost non-American, Nikita Khrushchev. His giant TU-114 plane has just landed. It came in just a few minutes earlier than we expected. However, the President was well informed. As he was supposed to, he arrived in his car just four minutes before the airplane landed. The giant plane is so big that the spread between its wheels prevented it from going in all the way to the apron of the field where the reception line is waiting. It will have to stop some distance away and the President will have to walk all the way out and welcome Khrushchev and then escort him into the receiving line.

Smith describes the plane in detail and identifies for viewers the scaffolding packed with reporters and photographers.

SMITH: A very small crowd is out here watching. Despite the security arrangements, anyone who wanted to come could come. They are required to park their cars some distance away, but the Air Force itself provided buses for any members of the public who wanted to come.

Now the President is going out to meet the plane with his three military aides

Familiar formalities

The first introduction

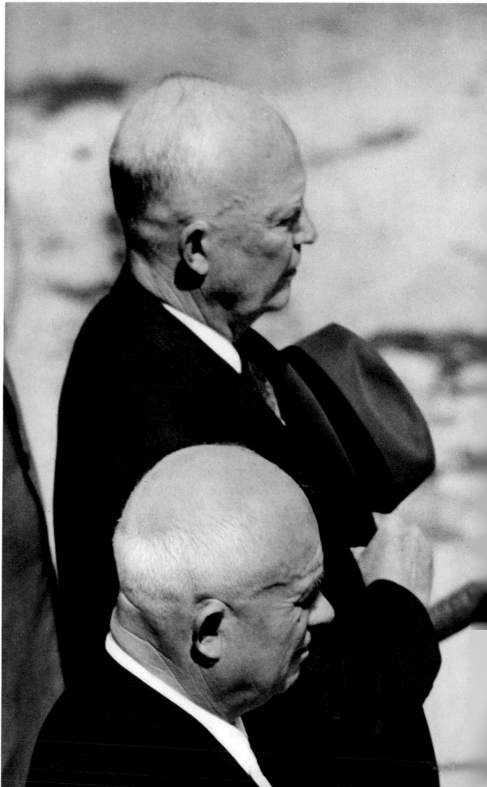

"Which so proudly we hail"

and an interpreter. The motors of the plane die down now and in just a moment the door will open and Chairman Khrushchev will come down.

The honor Guard has been ordered to attention . . . There are two signs in Russian letters welcoming Khrushchev. One of the signs says simply, "Welcome Khrushchev," the other says, "Khrushchev welcome to Washington." It may well be that these are the last two signs we will see friendly to Khrushchev. I understand that towards the center of the city there are some rather unfriendly ones. The band plays *Hail to the Chief* in honor of the President.

Now here are Premier Khrushchev and the President walking the long distance —about the length of a football field—and seeming to chat with animation as they go. Khrushchev waves his hat. They stop for a moment before photographers. Interpreters are right behind them, translating one to the other. These have been described as the two most expressive faces in world politics and they certainly appear to be so.

In January 1958 Secretary of State Dulles, in a speech at the National Press Club, stated that he was opposed to any such visit. He said it would constitute the greatest triumph for the Communist world.

". . . our people do want peace . . ."

Smith continues with a description of the introduction between Mr. Khrushchev and Secretary of State Herter, Ambassadors Henry Cabot Lodge and Llewellyn Thompson, General Nathan Twining and other government officials. The television audience sees Mr. and Mrs. Khrushchev escorted to the reviewing stand and the band plays the Soviet national anthem and *The Star Spangled Banner*.

SMITH: Behind the two leaders are the two foreign ministers who have spent fruitless days, weeks, and months in Geneva trying to negotiate problems and have failed completely, so now it's up to their bosses.

The President is showing Khrushchev the way to the microphones. And the President of the United States will now speak his words of greeting.

EISENHOWER: Mr. Chairman:

I welcome you, your family and party to the United States. I am especially happy that Mrs. Khrushchev and other members of your family are accompanying you.

On behalf of the Government and the people of America I express the hope that you and they will find your stay among us interesting and useful. I am looking forward to the talks we will have together.

Although we shall not be negotiating any issues affecting the interest of other countries, I trust that a full and frank exchange of views on many subjects may contribute to better understanding, on both sides, of unresolved international questions.

During your stay here you will have an opportunity to see something of our country, our institutions, our customs and our people. You will have a chance to speak with individuals and groups from all walks of life.

The political and social systems of our two countries differ greatly. In our sys-

Studio control room monitors

"...the pleasure of first meeting you..."

"we should live together in peace and friendship..."

tem the people themselves establish and control the government. You will find that they, like your people, want to live in peace with justice. Although they have built and maintained strong security forces, it is clear that because our people do want peace and because they are the decisive influence in the basic actions of our government, aggression by this nation is an impossibility.

Just as I hope that I may later visit and learn more about your people, I know that you seek better understanding of our system, of our people, and of the principles which guide and motivate them.

I assure you that they have no ill will toward any other people—that they covet no territory, no additional power, nor do they seek to interfere in the internal affairs of any other nation.

I most sincerely hope that as you come to see and believe these truths about our people there will develop an improved basis on which we can together consider the problems that divide us.

After all, our common purpose should be, as always, a just, universal and enduring peace. It is in this spirit, Mr. Chairman, that I greet you and welcome you to Washington and to the United States.

A touch of sun

At the conclusion of the President's remarks, Oleg Troyanovsky, one of the two official Soviet interpreters, proceeds with the translation. Behind the Russian words Smith's voice can be heard reporting that it has just been announced that for the first time in many years the Russians have not jammed American broadcasts to the Soviet Union. Troyanovsky completes his translation and Smith resumes:

SMITH: Now the Chairman of the Council of Ministers, Nikita Khrushchev, is going to speak.

KHRUSHCHEV: Mr. President, ladies and gentlemen:

Permit me at this moment, in first setting foot on American soil, to thank Mr. Eisenhower for the invitation to visit your country, and everyone present for the warm welcome accorded to us representatives of the Soviet Union.

Russians say every good job should be started in the morning. Our flight began in Moscow this morning and we now have the pleasure of first meeting you on American soil on the morning of the same day.

As you see our countries are not so distant from each other.

I accepted the invitation of the President of the United States to make an official visit to your country with great pleasure and gratitude, and I will be glad to meet and talk with your statesmen, representatives of the business world, intellectuals, workers and farmers, and to learn about the life of the industrious and enterprising American people.

For our part we will be glad to receive Mr. Eisenhower, his family and those who will shortly accompany him to the Soviet Union. We will give the President a most cordial welcome and every opportunity to become familiar with the life of the Soviet people...

The Soviet and the American people and the people of other countries fought

Arrival in Washington

Presenting arms

"Just courteous silence"

well together in the Second World War against the common enemy and broke his backbone. In peaceful conditions we have even more reasons for friendship and cooperation between the people of our countries...

In these first few minutes of our stay in the United States permit me to extend cordial greetings and best wishes to the American people on behalf of the Soviet Union, the Soviet Government and on my own behalf...

A tight squeeze

Shortly before this meeting with you, Mr. President, Soviet scientists, engineers, technicians and workers filled our hearts with joy by launching a rocket to the moon. A road thus has been laid from the earth to moon, and a container of 390 kilograms with a pennant bearing the national emblem of the Soviet Union is now on the moon. Our earth has become somewhat lighter while the moon has gained several hundred pounds in weight. I'm sure that this historic achievement of peaceful science has brought joy not only to the Soviet people but to all who cherish peace and friendship among nations. We have no doubt that the excellent scientists, engineers and workers of the United States of America who are engaged in the field of conquering the cosmos will also carry their pennant over the moon. The Soviet pennant, as an old resident, then will welcome your pennant and they will live there together in peace and friendship as we should live together in peace and friendship and as all people should live who inhabit our common mother earth...

For the next hour and a half a nationwide audience keeps its eyes on the President and the Premier as the ceremonies continue at the air base and the motorcade embarks on its pre-arranged route into Washington. As it disappears intermittently from sight the cameras switch to an interview with Captain Harold Renegar, the U.S. Air Force "courtesy" pilot assigned to accompany the Russian plane on its flight to the United States. Renegar describes some of the technical aspects of the plane. The camera now picks up CBS News correspondent Bernard Eisemann, speaking from the Roswell Garst farm in Coon Rapids, Iowa. Eisemann points out the main features of the farm and introduces its proprietor who is to play host to the Premier during his tour of the Midwest. Garst expresses his enthusiasm for the Soviet Premier's visit, hailing it as an example of a new turn in international relations which he calls the era of "full-bellied diplomacy."

By now the motorcade is crossing the South Capitol bridge and proceeding through Suitland Park. At their pre-assigned posts, CBS News correspondents report its arrival in downtown Washington. From his vantage point in the National Press Club, Bill Downs describes the

"A banner with a strange device"

Home away from home

*Gallantry
at the summit*

crowd as "sparse," giving an impression of more policemen and soldiers than spectators. He notes that a few people are wearing "mourning" armbands. Pierpoint reports a crowd of several thousand across from the White House . . . "a friendly crowd with a conspicuous number of baby carriages." He describes a plane tracing a huge white cross in the sky which he finds puzzling. (It remains an object of speculation until it is revealed as the work of a skywriter hired by an anti-Communist organization.) Pierpoint calls attention to a large sedan bearing a sign reading "No cheers, applause . . . just courteous silence."

A negative view

At the Agricultural Building von Fremd describes the crowd as "really quite fantastic . . . many hundreds of thousands," and reports that the President has ordered his chauffeur to slow down from the predetermined speed of 30 miles per hour in order that the crowds may get a better glimpse of the Premier. As the formal parade assembles at 14th Street and Independence Avenue the famous obelisk of the Washington Monument looms into sight.

". . . a conspicuous number of baby carriages"

The cameras now switch to Paul Niven, former CBS News Moscow correspondent, who takes note of Premier Khrushchev's expansive gestures to the milling crowds. "We old Moscow hands," he reports, "could hardly wait to see how long it would take for Khrushchev to start hamming it up." Niven refers to similar behavior on the part of the Soviet Premier during Vice President Nixon's trip to Moscow.

Daniel Schorr, Niven's predecessor in Moscow, picks up the narration to describe the final leg of the procession — the arrival at Blair House. As it passes the White House, Schorr reports that the President wants to make it a "field day" for the Premier and is not attempting "to take any of the play away from him." He reports that "Khrushchev seems to be having a fine time. Despite the elaborate security precautions, he seems to show no visible fear."

The television audience sees the Khrushchevs pose for photographs on the steps of Blair House and then disappear inside after bidding the President goodbye.

A present for the President—the Soviet moon rocket

A confident stride

CBS News Mobile Unit

In nearly eight million homes throughout the nation, housewives shut off their vacuum cleaners, left the kettle boiling on the stove, and cut short their telephone conversations to see what the Khrushchevs, man and wife, were like. They saw them individually and as a family—a jaunty, quick-smiling man, a grey-haired motherly-looking woman. They saw the two Khrushchev daughters, a son, and a son-in-law. They observed the way they conducted themselves under the pressure of an elaborate official reception.

By the time the visiting Russians left the screen, at least part of the veil surrounding one of the world's most enigmatic personalities had been lifted.

In mid-afternoon, CBS News broke into the network's schedule with a two-minute view of Khrushchev leaving Blair House with Vice President Nixon and Secretary Herter for his first official conference at the White House with President Eisenhower.

That night at 7:30 pm the CBS Television Network presents the fifth in its special series of half-hour news programs covering the travels of the President and the Premier.

Walter Cronkite opens the program by announcing that in "a few minutes from now the Premier of Soviet Russia in white tie and tails will enter the White House as guest of the President of the United States. The formal dinner at which the Eisenhowers of Washington entertain the Khrushchevs of Moscow is the final event of the day that is already marked as a date in history…the first time a chief of the Communist world has set foot on American soil."

Cronkite then describes the events of the Premier's arrival earlier in the day, and millions of working Americans who were unable to witness the proceedings at the time now have an opportunity to view the scenes at Andrews Air Force Base and the parade into Washington. Cronkite breaks into the picture to announce that the Premier and his party are about to leave for the Presidential dinner. The cameras switch to the doorway of Blair House.

CBS News covers the band

Ready to receive the guests

Two First Ladies

The receiving line

CRONKITE: You see the front door of Blair House open—and the Premier should be leaving there in a moment. A car is drawn up in front; actually, it's only 200 yards or so catty-corner across the street to the White House at 1600 Pennsylvania Avenue. But the Premier, of course, will drive in the limousine there, and it'll be a six-block drive around and into the side entrance at the White House. There is Premier Khrushchev and Madame Khrushchev. The Premier in white tie and tails; Madame Khrushchev in formal dress . . .

Cronkite fails to notice what millions of viewers observe: the Soviet Premier is *not* wearing formal dress but a dark business suit. Before the program closes, Cronkite makes the necessary correction.

Meanwhile, Schorr appears on the screen to sum up the significance of the Premier's first day in Washington:

Passengers: President and Premier

SCHORR: When Khrushchev entered the White House today he already completed half of his mission. He had planted in our capital the banner of Soviet equality with America; he had wrapped himself in the mantle of the great peacemaker who forced this exchange on a reluctant Eisenhower.

He's billed himself throughout Eastern Europe as the man who can end the "cold war," and if he doesn't it won't be his fault. All this is already paying him dividends. In Poland from where I've just come, he has won more popularity by coming to America than by touring Poland. And there's another big dividend. The Soviets are spreading the message that American acceptance of Khrushchev means the American acceptance of the Soviet domination of Eastern Europe. So, the satellites may be more ready to accept that domination too.

Now, comes part two, conquest of America itself. In Eastern Europe it is not expected that Khrushchev will make any real concessions on Berlin or any other major issue. On the contrary, one of his objectives is American agreement to keep hands off East Europe, of which he considers Berlin a part. He also wants more trade with America and disarmament, but he doesn't think he'll reach his specific goals overnight. He'll be satisfied for now if he can put across the twin points of overwhelming Soviet power and overwhelming Soviet desire for peace. He's not sure he can sell our leaders; he does think he's enough of a salesman to make an effective pitch over their heads to the American people.

In a private talk recently with Gomulka, the Polish Communist leader, Khrushchev gave a clue to his basic aims. He said the exchange visits with President Eisenhower are historic turning points. "You will see," he told Gomulka, "that in two or three years the 'cold war' will be over, and coexistence solidly established." Then, free of danger of war, Soviet military resources can be turned to economic expansion in competition with the West. Then, free of the danger of Western interference, the Communists can complete the consolidation and the economic integration of Eastern Europe. Khrushchev thinks the end of the "cold war" will be his great monument. Today as he enters the White House, a super-salesman selling only a better climate, he started on the mission of his lifetime, the psychological disarmament of America.

"It would be better if all nations concentrated on raising turkeys"

Chemically grown

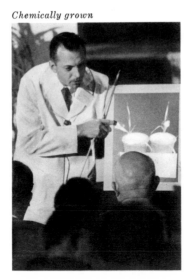

Taking stock

This was the composite picture of Mr. Khrushchev's first day in the United States that went into the homes of millions of Americans across the nation. Strenuous as it was, it still failed to dent what appeared to be the boundless energies of the Soviet Premier who was up, shaved and dressed by 7:30 am the next day and out on the front stoop of Blair House for a brief view of Washington in the early morning. The inevitable cameramen were there too, thus enabling millions of television viewers to see the picture of the beaming leader of the Communist world standing in the doorway of Blair House in his shirtsleeves and seeming to enjoy the attention he was getting.

Parade rest

Two hours later he set out for the Agricultural Research Center at Beltsville, Maryland to listen to scientists explain the use of chemicals in growing plants. Correspondent Neil Strawser and cameraman Bruce Hoertel were close behind. The Premier registered interest in the American method of dehorning cattle and visited the famous Beltsville turkey farm where he handled the birds with the ease and familiarity of a professional poultryman. It was here that he remarked that "it would be better if all nations concentrated on raising turkeys." It was here also that Mrs. Khrushchev, who had accompanied her husband on the tour, strayed from her guards and had difficulty in getting back to her car until a burly motorcycle policeman grasped her hand and bulldozed his way through the crowd.

Monitors at the National Press Club

The Premier returned to Washington to attend the luncheon given in his honor by the National Press Club, the Women's National Press Club and the Overseas Writers. His hour-long address and the concluding 40-minute question-and-answer period were broadcast over the CBS Television Network at 1:30 pm. It was during this address that he announced his intention to make an important proposal on disarmament the following day in his speech before the United Nations General Assembly in New York.

At the very opening of the question-and-answer period viewers got their first sight of the Premier's swiftly changing moods. He was asked

"Let each of us live

...under the system...we prefer

...you under capitalism, we under communism"

"I shall not reply to this question"

to comment on the possibly apocryphal story of his speech in Moscow at which a member of the audience submitted an unsigned question asking him what he had been doing "while Stalin was committing these crimes." According to the story, Khrushchev invited the anonymous questioner to stand up and identify himself. When there was no reaction, he replied "Now you know what I was doing."

Upon hearing the story retold, the Premier's face flooded with anger "I shall not reply to this question," he declared, "which I look upon as being provocative, and I would like to take this occasion to deny such malicious rumors and lies . . ." It was a different Khrushchev from the smiling, hat-waving, ingratiating visitor of the day before. However, anger quickly gave way to humor when someone asked him whether the Soviet Union now intends to claim possession of the moon. "I would say," he replied, "that this question reflects capitalist psychology—of a person thinking in terms of private ownership."

He concluded the question-and-answer period with an elaborate explanation of his frequently quoted phrase: "We will bury you," pointing out the inevitability of communism's victory over capitalism. Meanwhile, he said, "let each of us live under the system which we prefer, you under capitalism, and we will continue to build under communism."

Following the luncheon he continued on his tour of Washington, having time only to visit the Lincoln Memorial before meeting the members of the Senate Foreign Relations Committee in the Capitol.

In a special half-hour broadcast that night summarizing the events of the day, CBS News correspondent Howard K. Smith observed:

SMITH: Two different and contrasting views are crystallizing here as to the purpose of Mr. Khrushchev's visit. The U.S. view is that he is here primarily to see, to learn that his many misconceptions about us ought to be amended. But the Khrushchev view, it is becoming clear, is that he is here not so much to see as to be seen, to persuade us rather than to be persuaded himself. . . . Mr. Khrushchev came to life and became taut and conscientious and really extended himself only when he stopped seeing and stood up to be seen and heard at the Press Club today. He read that prepared speech, as you noticed, with marked deliberation, allowing himself no asides. He warned us that if he made any verbal mistakes to ask him again, for he wanted everything to be perfectly clear. He became, as you saw,

Smith summarizes

Arrival in New York—Baggage Room, Pennsylvania Station

Cronkite concentrates

A slight case of congestion

much more animated when answering questions and at one point became almost furious because he thought he was being misunderstood. His assumption appears to be that we simply don't understand him.

If we will only listen carefully to him in person now as in the case of that little lesson in Marxian history a moment ago it will all become clear to us and we will then agree with him. Few of his audience of reporters were able to share that assumption. The speech had nothing new of substance in it, but that's the way it should be on the eve of delicate private talks with the President. However, Mr. Khrushchev did convey one powerful impression to his audience. Prime Minister Macmillan of Britain, it seems, was right. Khrushchev and nobody else is in charge. He talked and looked like an extremely capable man, aware of his ability, a powerful man assured of his power. It became clear to us that if it is possible to get an agreement with Russia we have in our midst at last the one man who can give it.

Security check

Visibly unmarked by the frantic pace of his first days in America, the Premier and his party boarded a Pennsylvania Railroad train early Thursday morning, September 17, for two days in New York. These were to be equally crowded: a luncheon and reception by Mayor Wagner; a private meeting with 26 prominent business leaders at the town house of former Governor Averell Harriman; a dinner and speech before the Economic Club in the evening. The following day he was to spend the morning with Mrs. Roosevelt at Hyde Park and in the afternoon he was scheduled to address the General Assembly of the United Nations.

Sidewalks of New York

In the case of two of these events—the Harriman and Hyde Park visits—careful planning far in advance by CBS News enabled the network to gain a unique advantage in setting up its coverage facilities. It was comparable in a sense to that most prized of all journalistic achievements—the exclusive story. A month earlier CBS News reporter Sam Jaffe, through personal contacts with members of the Soviet Delegation to the U.N., had privately learned that the Premier had accepted invitations from Governor Harriman and Mrs. Roosevelt. Jaffe immediately requested and obtained permission from both of them to cover the events. Although the Harriman meeting was private the former Governor agreed to be interviewed by Walter Cronkite after the guests had departed. Mrs. Roosevelt acceded to a request to wear a portable wireless microphone while conducting Premier and Mrs. Khrushchev through

Mayor Wagner entertains

Inside Harriman's house

The line-up,
Waldorf-Astoria

the grounds of Hyde Park. The stage was set.

Viewers throughout the nation witnessed the Premier's arrival at noon at Penn Station on the network's 1 pm news program and again at night on *Douglas Edwards with the News*. They saw the motorcade speed through dense crowds to the Waldorf-Astoria Hotel and heard portions of the Premier's speech at the Wagner luncheon. That afternoon Cronkite obtained his interview with Mr. Harriman. It came at the close of Mr. Khrushchev's meeting at the former Governor's home in New York.

Guests of Mrs. Rockefeller and Mrs. Wagner

CRONKITE: Mr. Harriman, what did Mr. Khrushchev tell you today?

HARRIMAN: Well, I can't give you a detailed account. I'd rather have you get it directly from him. Of course, he can't see the difference between the Republican and Democratic parties, and he told that, of course, to the Foreign Affairs Committee, and he thinks we're ruled by one thought—it doesn't make much difference whether it's the Republicans or the Democrats. He also does seem to still have the impression there is a ruling circle, and there are some people in the United States that want to keep the war orders going, or I should say, the armament orders going. I hope that we've made an impression on him. The men who spoke showed great sincerity, and in view of that he's been impressed with the way they handled themselves.

Television cameras were excluded from the Economic Club dinner —another occasion at which the Premier again displayed his anger at what he considered improper heckling by members of the audience, threatening at one point to leave the banquet hall "if there is no desire to listen to what I have to say."

The following morning nearly three million viewers throughout the nation had the remarkable experience of being taken on a personally guided tour of the ancestral home and grounds of the late Franklin Delano Roosevelt by his widow. The day was overcast and there was a 40-minute delay in the arrival of the Khrushchevs. Under the supervision of Producer-Director Robert Quinn, five television cameras were stationed at strategic points inside and outside the main house, near the grave, and at the Roosevelt Memorial Library building about a quarter of a mile from the main house, together with the CBS News mobile unit and its recording and transmitting equipment. Two CBS News

"Will you stay right beside us as we talk together?"

A brief interview

A moment of tribute

correspondents – Charles Kuralt and Harry Reasoner – reported the events.

At 11:10 Mrs. Roosevelt and the Khrushchevs, surrounded by a jam of security police, reporters, photographers and official visitors, appear on the television screen. She is wearing the wireless microphone around her neck. Although her introductory remarks are fragmentary, they can be heard distinctly. Viewers have the sensation of eavesdropping on a private conversation:

Pause for affection

MRS. ROOSEVELT: How do you do. I'm so glad to see you. How do you do, Mr. Gromyko. May I introduce you to my son, John and his wife? Mr. Zhukov and Mrs. Gromyko... They are anxious to have a photograph. Could we have a clear space so they get their photograph? That's all. We turn to the right here. Are you all finished? Are you all finished?... No. No. No, we're not doing that because we're turning the other way. *(To Premier Khrushchev)* Will you stay right beside us as we talk together? Well, I am glad you've had a pleasant trip. It was too bad that it began to look so cloudy because we have had good weather. I would like to present Secretary Morgenthau. He was Secretary of the Treasury during my husband's administration... I've lost Mrs. Morgenthau... this is Mrs. Morgenthau.

A comment from CBS News Sam Jaffe

KURALT: Mrs. Roosevelt and the Khrushchev party are now approaching the tomb of President Roosevelt, almost a cortege, following in and making a semi-circle. Premier Khrushchev now is taking the wreath from two assistants, placing it on a stand directly in front of the tomb. That wreath must be a good four feet in diameter. Premier Khrushchev is now walking back to Mrs. Roosevelt and Mrs. Khrushchev and turning to face the grave. They're standing there in solemn silence for a moment. A great many people have come here to pay tribute to Franklin Delano Roosevelt but surely no visitor like this one before. Now he's walking around the tomb again, the tomb where President Roosevelt lies and where an inscription has already been made for Eleanor Roosevelt. Compared to most of what Premier Khrushchev has done so far in America this is an informal, uncrowded occasion. Mrs. Roosevelt lent the informal neighborly tone right at the beginning. For once Nikita Khrushchev seems dominated. Mrs. Roosevelt has him by the arm and is obviously in charge. The party will now go to the house.

MRS. ROOSEVELT: *(To the interpreter)* I think it might be of interest to Mr. Khrushchev to know that the reason my husband's grave is in front of the monument is because he wanted to lie with no stone over him, with the sky above him. It might also interest him to know that this old pine tree was the one that all of the children always climbed, and my husband used to build boards as he got older and older, in the trees, and always called them ships, and he used to study his stamps and then he could sail to the places where the ships would take him to, in that tree there. That's how as a little boy he knew so much about geography.

Addressing the General Assembly of the United Nations

Catching the television signal

CBS News' director, John Day, Video Tape Room

And this was the house we used to live in. He was born in this house but he added the whole end for a library.

The main house becomes visible and Kuralt describes its rooms and contents: the late President's knicknacks, naval prints, grandfather clocks and so on. Viewers follow Mrs. Roosevelt and the Khrushchevs to the library building where CBS News has a camera in the study. After entering the study the Premier examines some of the correspondence between Stalin and President Roosevelt. He seems grave and restrained, "with the air of a man," reports Reasoner, "who knows how to act in the presence of important old ladies."

Full attendance, full attention

MRS. ROOSEVELT: We thought you would like to sit down. Madame Khrushchev, perhaps you would like to sit over there . . . if you would sit down . . . these are just things that were in the archives we thought you might like to see, and will you both sign your names . . . I beg your pardon . . . and you sign also, after her.

REASONER: That was all at Hyde Park. The feeling seemed to be as at Lincoln's Tomb, that Khrushchev was impressed, or finds it politic to be impressed by historical Americans not now in office.

Increasingly large audiences were able to catch the uniquely intimate flavor of the events at Hyde Park as segments of the program were broadcast on the network's various news programs throughout the day and night.

At 3 pm that afternoon the Soviet Premier launched on his hour-and-a-half address before the General Assembly of the United Nations—an event that, in the eyes of many political observers, was the climactic and primary purpose of his visit to the United States. In his speech he proposed complete and general disarmament of all nations within four years. It was carried in full over the CBS Television Network.

With the Premier's departure Saturday morning by jet for California, CBS News entered the second phase of its coverage of the Khrushchev visit, applying essentially the same procedures that characterized the Washington and New York operations. A Central News Desk was established at the network's affiliated stations in each of the principal centers of activity with a CBS News administrator or producer in charge. A constant two-way flow of communication was maintained be-

Assistant CBS News Director Johnson, Studio 44, New York

Like back home in Baku

Arrival, Los Angeles

tween each Desk and the Central News Room in New York where the major assignments originated. From this headquarters a variety of orders radiated out to the News Desks and thence to the correspondents and cameramen—orders for special newsfilm stories for syndication, two-minute tape recordings for radio and television dissemination, extended "wrap-ups" of the day's events for inclusion in the special half-hour *Eyewitness To History* programs. Prior to the Premier's arrival in the United States nearly 9300 miles of sound-and-picture carrying cables as well as microwave facilities, crisscrossing the nation, had been ordered from the American Telephone & Telegraph Company for use in transmitting the hundreds of thousands of electronic images and tens of thousands of words that would record the Prime Minister's activities.

From the moment of his arrival in California a distinct change could be noted in the atmosphere of the tour. The mood of restrained cordiality which had greeted him in the East gave way to a spirit of irritability and acrimony—created primarily by two factors: what seemed to be an excessive emphasis on security arrangements that reached a climax in the Disneyland incident; and an increasing tendency on the part of business, political and labor leaders to reflect unfavorably on the Soviet system in comparison with our own.

The heckling started at the glittering luncheon Saturday noon in the 20th Century-Fox Studio commissary, where the Premier met some 500 of Hollywood's shining stars including Marilyn Monroe, Deborah Kerr and Maurice Chevalier. In a special nationwide broadcast over the network Sunday night viewers witnessed the testy exchange between Spyros Skouras, president of the motion picture company, and the guest of honor.

In his introduction Skouras paid tribute to the American economic system that enabled him, "a poor immigrant boy," to achieve success after starting to work at the age of 12. The Premier took umbrage at what he regarded as the implied contrast to communism:

Geiger food check

Her head between the stars

"Just imagine, I, a Prime Minister

... could not go to Disneyland"

KHRUSHCHEV: *(as translated)* What you said about working since you were 12 certainly produces a very great impression ... But you can't surprise me by that, because if you want to know who I am, I started working as soon as I learned how to walk. Until the age of 15 I worked as a shepherd ... I herded cows for a capitalist ... After that I worked at a factory for a German. Then I worked in a French-owned mine. I worked at a Belgian-owned chemical factory. And I am the Prime Minister of the great Soviet State *(laughter and applause)*...

SKOURAS: How many Prime Ministers in Russia?

KHRUSHCHEV: How many Presidents are there in the United States? *(laughter)* ... We have a Prime Minister of the Central Government. I represent him. We also have 15 union republics ... That makes ... 15 more prime ministers. We have autonomous republics. They each have their own Prime Minister. Do you have that many? *(laughter)*

SKOURAS: We have 2,000,000 American presidents of American corporations. *(laughter)*

"That's a monopoly"

At this point the Premier asked a member of his party, a Mr. Tikhonov, to rise and identify himself. The Premier described him as a "worker," an administrator of metallurgical plants, mines and chemical factories, and suggested that the United States had no men richer than he. Turning to Mr. Skouras, the Premier remarked:

KHRUSHCHEV: Well, Comrade Greek, is that not enough for you?

SKOURAS: No. That's a monopoly. *(laughter)*

The colloquy continued for several minutes until it fell of its own weight. The Premier then turned to the question of security measures and the Disneyland incident.

KHRUSHCHEV: Just imagine I, a Prime Minister, a Soviet representative, when I came here to the city I was given a plan, a program, of what I was to be shown and whom I was to meet here. But just now I was told that I couldn't go to Disneyland. I asked why not. What is it you have ... rocket launching pads there? *(laughter)* And just listen, just listen to what I was told, to what reason I was told. "We,—which means the American authorities—cannot guarantee your security if you go there." What is it? Is there an epidemic of cholera or something? Or have gangsters taken hold of the place that can destroy me? Your policemen are so tough they can lift up a bull by the horns ... and surely they can restore order if there are any gangsters around. And I say I would very much like to go and see Disneyland.

Instead of Disneyland, the Khrushchevs were taken to the sound stage of a studio to watch a movie production in process—a rehearsal of a can-can dance by a line of 16 chorus girls and boys. At the time the

A word from Anita Louise

Another from Shirley MacLaine

A friendly hand from Frankie

"Humanity's face is more beautiful . . ."

Premier was reported as seeming interested and appreciative, although the following morning he appeared to have changed his mind, referring to the dance as pornographic, and asserting that "a man of normal morals is not interested in such things. Humanity's face is more beautiful than its backside."

On the network's special half-hour news program Sunday night viewers witnessed the proceedings at the dinner given by Mayor Norris Poulson and the World Affairs Council of Los Angeles. Here again Mr. Khrushchev displayed a burst of temper when Mayor Poulson raised the famous issue of the Premier's statement alleging that communism would "bury" capitalism.

An observation by Niven

KHRUSHCHEV: The unpleasant thought sometimes creeps up on me as to whether perhaps Khrushchev was not invited here to enable you to sort of rub him in your sauce and to show the might and the strength of the United States so as to make him shaky at the knees. If that is so, then if it took me about twelve hours to get here, I guess it'll take no more than about ten and a half hours to fly back.

CRONKITE: It is clear that Khrushchev is deeply disturbed at what he considers the needling he's receiving so far and he's annoyed also at the security guard which he thinks strangles his attempts to get his messages to the people. Tonight comes word that the State Department has itself become alarmed over his reaction, fearful that it will cloud the atmosphere when he sits down to talk with President Eisenhower next weekend. From Washington word has gone out to officials on his itinerary suggesting they ease up a bit, not perhaps just to salve Mr. Khrushchev's personal feelings, but to try to salvage something more out of this American tour.

During an interlude in the speeches correspondent Daniel Schorr, formerly stationed in Moscow for CBS News until denied a re-entry permit by Soviet authorities, advanced toward the dais and chatted briefly with the Premier with whom he had toured the U.S.S.R., Finland, Czechoslovakia, and Poland. Still smarting from his exchanges with Skouras and Poulson, Khrushchev remarked to Schorr, "You were better treated than this in Moscow." Schorr replied that he'd like to be back there again as a working correspondent. Khrushchev, he reported, nodded in approval. (Two months later the CBS News Bureau in Moscow, headed by Larry LeSueur, was reopened.)

The eagerness with which the Premier greeted Schorr supported the

En route to the dining car: an exclusive interview

Whistle-stop

Keeping order

frequent reports of his accessibility and responsiveness to the newsmen covering his travels. The difficulties which they encountered—and they were formidable—appeared to arise primarily from the security restrictions imposed on the Premier by his protectors, both American and Soviet. He himself seemed to have no fears of the possible dangers envisaged by those assigned to guard him. He seemed principally amused, according to Schorr, by the spectacle of a free press in action. No such behavior, Schorr reported, would be tolerated in the Soviet Union, where it would be regarded as somewhat impolite to a distinguished visitor to permit reporters and cameramen to practically suffocate him with their presence. They would be kept at their distance. To Khrushchev the behavior of the news media in a democracy seemed a form of anarchy—a form, incidentally, which he was quick to exploit by playing off one reporter against another, handing out brief interviews, now to newspapermen, now to television reporters, "mugging" for the nearest available cameraman, and hugely enjoying the entire process.

Noise-shielding lip "mike"

It was this same disregard for personal security and delight in confronting newsmen that enabled CBS News correspondent Grant Holcomb to obtain an exclusive filmed interview with the Premier on the train to San Francisco Sunday morning. Observing the Premier and Ambassador Lodge walking through the train corridor towards the dining car, Holcomb and cameraman Fred Dieterich planted themselves firmly between the two cars, thus effectively blocking the Premier's passage. Late viewers watched a portion of the interview on the network's *Sunday News Special* program at 11 pm.

HOLCOMB: Mr. Chairman, how do you like your train trip so far?

KHRUSHCHEV: It's a wonderful train. It's a comfortable ride. Wonderful view . . . we are very pleased.

HOLCOMB: Speaking of views, did you enjoy your trip through Vandenberg Air Base?

KHRUSHCHEV: I was especially pleased. I don't know for how long the house arrest I was placed under will be lifted. I was allowed to alight from the car and approach the people and look them in the eye.

HOLCOMB: Does that "house arrest" refer to Disneyland, Mr. Chairman?

The familiar gesture

Russian translation

"It was a very interesting afternoon"

KHRUSHCHEV: Not only that, I was not allowed to go anywhere. The only thing I was allowed to do was eat and go to sleep.

LODGE: *(interrupting)* And you didn't do much of that.

KHRUSHCHEV: They fed us well.

HOLCOMB: Where are some of the places you would like to have gone, Mr. Chairman?

KHRUSHCHEV: I was very pleased with having been allowed to alight from the car in Santa Barbara to see the people, and I was grateful to the Mayor for that possibility. They are a very fine people, and like all people, they want peace and friendship.

HOLCOMB: But that wasn't my question, Mr. Chairman. I said, "Where are some of the places you would like to have gone?"

KHRUSHCHEV: You want to ask your own questions; I want to give my own answers.

A trip down the Bay

At this point the Premier broke off the interview and proceeded to the dining car.

On Monday night at 10 the eighth special broadcast in the *Eyewitness To History* series gave viewers a composite picture of the Soviet Premier's two days in California. It included a brief, if somewhat static, interview with Marilyn Monroe concerning her reactions following the Los Angeles luncheon:

INTERVIEWER: From an entertainer's point of view, what do you think of the show today?

MARILYN MONROE: It was a very interesting afternoon.

INTERVIEWER: What did you find most interesting?

MARILYN MONROE: Nearly everything.

INTERVIEWER: What did you think of the ad libs?

MARILYN MONROE: Interesting.

INTERVIEWER: Eh?

MARILYN MONROE: Very interesting.

INTERVIEWER: What did you come expecting?

MARILYN MONROE: I expected it to be interesting.

The San Francisco sojourn was reported by correspondents Strawser and Niven:

STRAWSER: San Francisco, the city of cable cars and hills, has turned out to be the city of hospitality for Khrushchev, thanks mostly to his own bitter complaints about his reception elsewhere. And the Premier is reacting like the politician he is, even to the arms-over-the-head gesture; doing the unexpected; breaking away

Lamb chops, 90¢, lb.

Canteloupe, 29¢ ea.

*A new cap, a fresh bouquet
and some longshoremen*

to meet people; campaigning especially hard in the ranks of business and labor as he has been in the past twenty-four hours. At a private dinner last night the Premier didn't do so well with a group of labor leaders headed by Walter Reuther who reported a bitter clash as Khrushchev evaded their pointed questions. But Khrushchev did better in an unscheduled visit to Harry Bridges' Longshore Union Hall this morning. He accepted a longshoreman's cap, gave his own fedora in return, called it "an exchange of peace." Then, with the controversial Bridges looking on, Khrushchev drew warm praise from the crowd, declaring that the workers of America want peace as much as the workers of the Soviet Union want peace. "But peace is not enough," he said. He played directly to the workers, "I want work and a good wage." Then a long drive to Palo Alto to see the International Business Machines plant, incidentally a non-union plant. Here too, as the guest of IBM President Thomas J. Watson, Jr. and in the company of his executives Khrushchev seemed to do well. The first stop was the plant cafeteria where the Premier served himself.

IBM plant, Palo Alto

There was some puzzlement but he seemed to do nearly as well as any American faced with the mysteries of a new cafeteria, selecting chicken and french fries in a basket. He did not, of course, stop at the cash register. Other executives joined him and Khrushchev pitched in with gusto; finally wound up praising the capitalistic company president for his judgment in bringing him to the cafeteria first. Note the mildness of his talk.

KHRUSHCHEV: You've started off this acquaintance of mine with your plant by taking me to this dining room and you fed me so very well. You will know, of course, that even if you give an animal some good food an animal becomes kinder. *(laughter)* We too are using this method of catering but not to an adequate extent as yet, and this certainly is an example worthy of emulation by a socialist enterprise, too.

STRAWSER: Khrushchev went on to say that he finds he gets along very well with capitalistic company presidents in this country. They understand each other. That was, as he remarked, something of a phenomenon; but the unexpected is to be expected on this trip. And the next unexpected event came shortly after his return to San Francisco. The Premier suddenly found time to visit a supermarket much to the distress of security officials who had carefully prepared the way to another market he was to visit in the morning. For a time Khrushchev looked quietly, asked prices of food items. He talked there to store employees still on his campaign until police found it no longer possible to handle the crowd and hustled him away, still campaigning.

NIVEN: Two observations may be made about Khrushchev's behavior so far. The first is that he can smile and wave back when people smile and wave at him, and that he shows no sign of giving an inch on basic political issues. The second observation stems from that dinner meeting last night with seven labor leaders. This was the first time during the trip that Khrushchev had talked politics on a give-and-take basis with anybody. The conversation ranged from Hungary to disarmament, to censorship, to the can-can Khrushchev had seen in Hollywood, which he imitated and again described as immoral.

"Our positions were completely irreconcilable"—Reuther

CBS News' Bassow and friend

Cronkite reports a "new mellow mood"

AFL-CIO Vice President Walter Reuther presided because President George Meany boycotted the affair. Reuther said afterwards, "Our positions were completely irreconcilable." For his part Khrushchev described the union chiefs as capitalist lackeys. This may amuse the capitalists of Detroit who have periodically to deal with Mr. Reuther. But the general disharmony, even distemper, that prevailed, does not bode well for the Camp David talks with President Eisenhower this weekend. On the other hand, Mr. Eisenhower and others warned us before Khrushchev came that he was not going to be converted to the American way of life.

Iowa billboard welcomes Khrushchev

CRONKITE: The White House today took its first official notice of the needling and tried to apply a brake to it. A special White House message said, in effect, break it up, the needles won't help when the time comes for Khrushchev to face Eisenhower this weekend. The actual language of that statement: "The purpose of constructive meetings at Camp David is not served by any personal discourtesies extended to the Chairman during his visit."

We'll switch now to Washington for more on the Capital's feelings about this aspect of the tour, to CBS News correspondent Howard K. Smith.

Television down on the farm

SMITH: Washington where, or near where, the climax of Khrushchev's trip will be played in a few days, has watched the Soviet leader's tour pass the halfway mark with mixed feelings. There is, as the White House statement said today, a profound wish that Khrushchev will be treated courteously on his tour. It would be a shame if relations between the giant nuclear nations which survived the Berlin blockade and the Korean War now founder on a missed excursion to the Disneyland Amusement Park. Washington wants nothing to happen which would cast a shadow on the talks Khrushchev is to have with President Eisenhower here late this week. However, official Washington does not think that Khrushchev has been as badly treated as he has made out.

His plans and arrangements were made at the request of his own embassy and were rather different from what the State Department wanted him to do, which was to see a little more of Americans and America than he has been seeing.

On Tuesday the television audience witnessed the events of Khrushchev's first day in the Midwest. Cronkite reports that the Prime Minister is in a "new mellow mood," the result of his friendly reception by the people of San Francisco. A brief man-in-the-street interview in Des Moines appears on the screen revealing the familiar mixture of opinion concerning the Premier's visit to the United States, ranging from enthusiasm to apathy. Viewers follow Khrushchev's inspection of a meat-packing plant. Standing shoulder to shoulder with CBS News correspondent Harry Reasoner in the sausage department, the Prime Minister is given the first frankfurter of his trip. Reasoner, microphone in

Meat inspection

Farm machinery workers

"OK"

hand, is dressed in the standard white coat worn by the plant's employees. The network's cameras pick up the Premier as he takes a big bite and pronounces it excellent. Later he visits a farm implement factory. Viewers obtain another preview of Roswell Garst, who will entertain the Khrushchevs at his farm in Coon Rapids the next day. He is interviewed by CBS News correspondent Bernard Eisemann.

A fistful of corn

EISEMANN: What do you think you'd like to show him on your farm?

GARST: I'll show him, first, an Iowa corn crop that is something. Iowa this year produced the most bushels of corn of any state in all of history. Somewhere about 700 million bushels. And I'll show him the way we mechanize our corn and I'll show him how we mechanize cattle-feeding and how we've mechanized hog-feeding and show him how fewer people can raise more food with complete mechanization.

EISEMANN: Do you get the idea that he knows pretty well what the United States is about?

GARST: I think he knows all about the productiveness of the United States, and I think his misconception is largely one of thinking that large corporations in the United States are interested in war and preparation for war in the hopes of greater profits. Complete misconception. I think it's the greatest basic danger in the world that he thinks that the larger corporations are interested in war.

EISEMANN: I guess then you'll be wanting to talk to him about something other than farming when he does get here.

GARST: Primarily I want to talk to him about the importance of reduced armaments, not only here but in the Soviet Union, so that the world can get on with the business of living. Actually, with the explosion in population—twenty-five or thirty more million people in the world every year—the primary job of the world ought to be better food. And I can't help but think that well-fed people are less likely to be quarrelsome people than underfed people.

On September 23, 1959, the tiny farming community of Coon Rapids (pop. 1,700) doubles in size and becomes the center of the universe as the Soviet Premier and his party followed by its retinue of security police, news correspondents, public officials, national and international personalities, converge on its dusty crossroads and corn fields. During the preceding weeks, the Garst farm had become an electronic forest, interlaced with cables, mobile recording and transmitting units, microwave relay equipment, walkie-talkies, television cameras and microphones hanging from virtually every tree surrounding the main house and outbuildings. CBS News has installed video and audio lines near a

Some agricultural questions

As tall as the corn

*"O beautiful for spacious skies,
for amber waves of grain"*

"Now you fellows wait ..."

"... I cannot let you in ..."

"... the first guy that gets in ..."

huge oak tree and has commandeered the only telephone on the premises.

In millions of homes across the country Americans who tuned in their sets to the CBS Television Network that night shared in the excitement. This is what they saw as Cronkite set the scene:

CRONKITE: The visit started at one of the subsidiary farms. Even before he arrived there Khrushchev announced, "This is going to be a jovial day." He proceeded to live up to that forecast though at some points he did it under some pressure. What he saw of American farm land and American farm life during the first couple of hours is somewhat questionable. What he saw mostly was a stirring mass of reporters and cameramen that pressed in on him from all sides as he watched a harvester in action. They trampled the Garst corn and they got on the Garst nerves as he angrily let them know.

The "stirring mass" now takes over the television screen. Garst's nerves are showing:

GARST: Gentlemen, if you fellows will get back so we can see something maybe you can get a picture. Are you going to do this or aren't you going to do it? If you fellows will get back we'll give you some pictures. If you don't well you'd just as well quit. I want to show him . . . Now you fellows wait a minute. Whoa. If you fellows wait a minute, I'll tell you a story. I cannot . . . I cannot let you in the cattle lot because if I let you in the cattle lot we wouldn't have any cattle. So Steve, if you would just get Lars or one of the boys to get a club and get over by the gate the first guy that gets in the cattle lot we leave because the cattle will leave if you get in with us.

CRONKITE: It was 50 miles away, down the road a piece, that the main event of the day took place, a picnic lunch, and this is the menu, at Roswell Garst's white clapboard farmhouse. Khrushchev arrived well fortified with a breakfast of fruit juice, poached trout, roast loin of veal, vegetables, bread and a kind of pancake called blintzes . . The Garsts invited about 100 persons out to the picnic lunch at poolside and Khrushchev seemed genuinely pleased at meeting them, some of them neighbors, others prominent personalities . . That's Mr. Khrushchev, Mrs. Khrushchev, Mr. Garst of course. That's Mrs. Garst over on the left. She's introducing one of their six grandchildren. That one, I believe, is Eddie, six years old. He's got a couple of teeth missing.

CBS News correspondent Harry Reasoner corners the Premier and Mr. Garst.

REASONER: Mr. Khrushchev, do you think that Mr. Garst has put you in a good mood for Camp David?

KHRUSHCHEV: He has been creating that mood ever since we met in the Crimea with Mikoyan and Mr. Garst and myself. We had a good talk there.

GARST: However, as I tell him, we still haven't settled the problems. It's a little difficult when the diplomats get there. *(laughter)*

The Premier tells the Governor

CBS News cameraman Hoffman

Mrs. Garst entertains

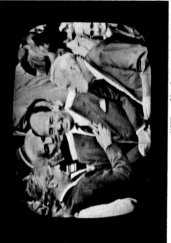

"We talked for a long time"

Next stop, Pittsburgh

Reasoner's interview is followed on the screen with one by Howard K. Smith with Garst and former Governor Adlai Stevenson, one of the many prominent personalities who have turned up at the scene.

SMITH: Governor Stevenson, I understand you had quite a chat with him. What did you talk about?

STEVENSON: Well, we talked for a long time. We talked about disarmament, we talked about what he'd seen in the United States and what he had learned and what he thought maybe we had learned from him. We talked about compassion cases, we talked about joint efforts and help in research. We talked about a great many things.

SMITH: The most important thing you enumerated is what he learned on his trip. What did he learn on his trip?

STEVENSON: I think Mr. Garst's view of this would probably be much more accurate than mine, but I think he will leave this country with a more profound conviction of America's hunger for peace than he had when he came.

SMITH: Did you talk to him about these matters too, Mr. Garst?

GARST: Certainly. Of course.

SMITH: Could you tell us what you said to him?

GARST: Yeah, I said . . . I told him that I thought the burden of armaments rested more heavily on the Soviet Union than it did on the United States. That we spent 10 per cent of our luxuries on defense; he spends 18 per cent of necessities in many cases.

SMITH: How did he take that?

GARST: Why, he agreed thoroughly this was true. And I told him I thought commentators, including yourself, have been pessimistic about making the sale, of having him accept inspection. I think actually that the odds of making this kind of a sale are greatly in our favor because he admits that the arms burden is more pressing on them than us, and I make fun of fellows like you, who take such a pessimistic attitude. I'm astonished . . .

SMITH: Now, *I'm* interviewing you, Mr. Garst. (*laughter*)

GARST: But, I'm astonished, actually at the general pessimism about his acceptance of a real inspection.

SMITH: And, do you think he will now agree to inspection, to real inspection?

GARST: I think he might have always done so had salesmanship been tried. And I talked to Mr. Lodge along these same lines, and I thought he made good sense.

SMITH: Well, that's good news. This is the right time for you to say that to him on the eve of the Camp David talks.

Pittsburgh was the next stop on the Premier's itinerary, the last before his return to Washington and his two-day conference with Presi-

105

Two at a time: Mesta steel works

A good cigar

An extra wristwatch

A makeshift emblem

dent Eisenhower at Camp David. He arrived at his hotel about Wednesday midnight to find CBS News' Sam Jaffe stationed at the entrance with a camera crew. Despite the lateness of the hour he acceded to a brief interview before retiring. The following afternoon he gave a speech at the University of Pittsburgh after an introduction by Governor Lawrence of Pennsylvania. In his introduction, Lawrence pointed out that he himself, although a Democrat, stood firmly behind President Eisenhower's foreign policy, pointing out that in this area there is no difference between parties. This remark won immediate agreement from the Premier, who said that he could never tell the difference between the two American political parties anyway. In the Soviet Union, he pointed out, there is only one party "but it's better than both of yours." He added, however, that the Russian people stood behind this party in the same way that Americans stood behind the President. He reported that before he left Moscow, people said to him, "Khrushchev, go to America. Strive for peace. But stand firmly on your own feet."

At the conclusion of his address the Premier left immediately for Washington and the Soviet Embassy dinner. On the eleventh and final special program of the *Eyewitness to History* series, viewers watched the events in Pittsburgh including the Premier's visit to the steel plant where he drank a toast in Coca-Cola with a machinist, gave a worker his wrist watch in exchange for a cigar, and invited the plant manager to visit him in Moscow—as he put it, in order to give the Khrushchev grandchildren a chance to see "a real live capitalist." Scenes at the Soviet Embassy reception followed and CBS News correspondent Howard K. Smith summed up the events.

SMITH: The most fantastic tour in America since Captain John Smith taught the leaves of Virginia to talk has now come to an end. As you've just seen, the last big social occasion of the tour is going on here inside the Soviet Embassy in Washington. As the diplomatic part of the Khrushchev visit is about to begin people here have begun trying to assess what the tour part has produced and here are some speculations. If Mr. Khrushchev has spoken truthfully, two important changes of the Soviet Communist line may have taken place. Hitherto Communist propaganda has said that capitalist America cannot stop the arms race with-

The entrance to Camp David

"Just one more, please"

"That's enough"

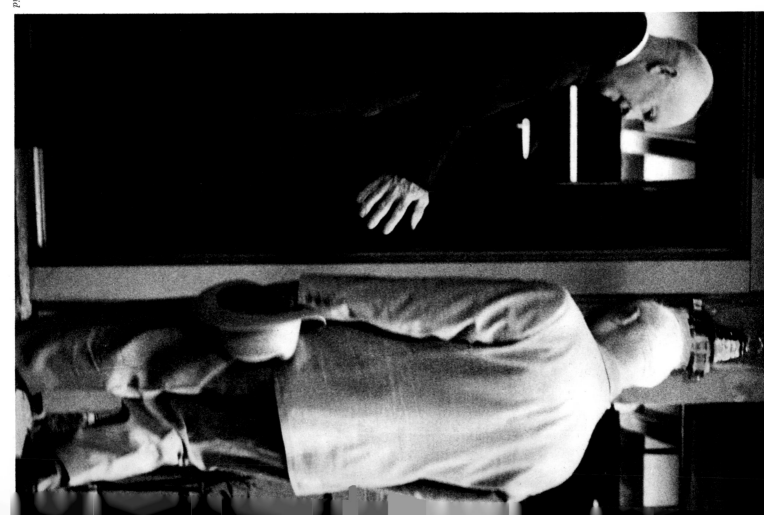

Final press conference

out having an economic crisis. Yesterday in Iowa Mr. Khrushchev told Governor Stevenson that he disavowed that. He thought the United States could shift without trouble from arms production . . . Another possible result of the tour is that Mr. Khrushchev may have strengthened his position in the Communist hierarchy at home against internal competitors. The Soviet people have, apparently, a great appetite for peace and friendship and Khrushchev by this trip has appeared to do more to appease it than any past Soviet leader has . . . These are possible results. However, they are all speculation. The strongest probability is that the tour's success or failure will really depend on the talks about to begin at Camp David. If those talks go badly, the tour has been bad; if they go well, the whole tour including the can-can exhibition, the failure to see Disneyland, and the whole super-security measures will be judged a howling success.

On Friday Premier Khrushchev and President Eisenhower left Washington for their two-day conference at Camp David. It was a closed meeting and the burden of the discussion was not made public until the following Sunday afternoon at the Premier's final press conference in Washington at 4 pm where CBS News correspondents Daniel Schorr and Sam Jaffe were among the questioners. The conference had no sooner begun when word came through from the White House that President Eisenhower had decided to postpone his visit to the Soviet Union until next Spring. CBS News interrupted three professional football games then being broadcast on the network in different sections of the country with a bulletin announcing the President's decision. At the press conference Jaffe had also heard about it and asked the obvious but necessary question :

JAFFE: What reason did President Eisenhower give you for postponing his visit to Russia until Spring?

KHRUSHCHEV: I would like to reveal a secret, although I have not asked the President's permission. But he said he would follow me on television and I will allow myself to say this happened.

Yesterday the President was kind enough to invite me to his farm, where I met his wonderful grandchildren. I established direct contact with those wonderful grandchildren of his and we held a conference with them as to whether they should accompany their grandfather to our country, and if so, when.

At that conference with the President's grandchildren they and I reached a unanimous decision that they certainly should come with the President.

The question of time arose, and I took it upon myself to suggest that perhaps springtime would be the best time of the year for a visit like that, because everything is in flower then, the weather is warm, nothing is frozen up. And then

Some concluding words

The last goodbye

Bon voyage

Nixon speaks Russian

we had an exchange of views with the President and came to the same conclusion. So there is no point in looking for fleas where fleas do not exist.

If I have revealed something which I shouldn't have revealed, I ask the President to excuse me.

I am sure that my grandchildren would approve of this action of mine, and therefore there is agreement both among the grandchildren and among the grandfathers.

During the conference the Premier reported generally on the Camp David discussions. He said that the President and he had reached agreement on several issues: that all major international problems should be settled by negotiation rather than force; that a specific attempt would be made to negotiate the Berlin issue; and that certain other agreements were likely to follow with respect to trade between the two countries and the further exchange of persons and ideas; finally, that the President's anticipated trip to the Soviet Union would be arranged through diplomatic channels.

At 6 o'clock, the CBS Television Network broadcast a half-hour digest of the conference. At 10 pm the network's television cameras were in position at Andrews Air Force Base as Premier Khrushchev and his party were about to enter the giant TU-114 turbo-prop airliner to return home.

Vice President Nixon and Secretary Herter were on hand to speed the departing guest. The television audience witnessed the final good-byes.

NIXON: Mr. Chairman, when you arrived in our country thirteen days ago, there were some basic differences, great differences between our two nations and our two governments. As you leave our country today, as the communique which you and President Eisenhower issued has indicated, these differences still exist. But we also believe that your visit here and the meetings you have had with our President can be a significant step toward establishing a pattern through which these differences can be settled by peaceful means. We all know that where two great nations like ours are concerned, where we are both strong and where we have differences, that the use of force to settle them is unthinkable.

If we are to settle them by peaceful means, we know too that the objective will be served if our leaders know each other. It will be served if each respects the strength and determination of the other. It will be served if our leaders talk with each other. And your visit here has served all of these objectives.

May I say as you leave our country you will take with you the hopes, the

"Until we meet again"

prayers of all the American people for the great cause of peace and friendship between all peoples on this earth. . . .

And so, with that, we wish you a safe journey, and we hope that you will extend to your people from our people the feelings for peace which I know you sensed every place that you went. *Do svidaniya, vse khorosho.* (Goodbye, may everything turn out for the best.)

CRONKITE: And now Nikita Khrushchev's final statement made on American soil.

KHRUSHCHEV: Mr. Nixon, and ladies and gentlemen, our stay in the United States is now coming to an end. We were here at the kind invitation of President Eisenhower. We visited various cities in your country from the Atlantic to the Pacific. We had many pleasant meetings and talks with Americans, with the business people of America, with political and public men. We met your workers, farmers and intellectuals. As a result of the useful talks we had with President Eisenhower, we came to an agreement that all outstanding international issues should be settled not through the use of force but by peaceful means and through negotiations. When we come home we shall tell the Soviet people of our impressions, of the meetings and talks we had on American soil. The Soviet people as a whole seek to live in peace. They want there to be good friendly relations between our two great nations. We are convinced that the American people also desire peace. There are many outstanding issues between us. But let us rather not turn to the past but look to the future and do all we can for that future. Let us join efforts to consolidate peace and to improve understanding between all the nations of the world.

From the bottom of my heart I want to express my gratitude for your kind hospitality, for your bread and salt, as they say in our country. I hope that in the relationships between our two countries we will be able to use more and more often the good, short American word: OKAY. Until we meet again, friends.

The two men shook hands. The Soviet Premier, with Mrs. Khrushchev, climbed the ramp leading into the plane and disappeared from view.

EPILOGUE: *Flashing its pictures on the home screen at the standard rate of 30 frames per second, the CBS Television Network presented to the nation's viewers a total of 1,793,010 separate electronic images depicting the travels of President Eisenhower in Western Europe and Premier Khrushchev in the United States.*

They were transmitted in the course of 78 news broadcasts in which 27 CBS News correspondents appeared 121 times. Approximately 38 million American families witnessed one or more of these broadcasts and on the average spent two hours and twenty minutes watching them.

It may occur to some who saw these images to revert to the original question: Was it worth it? We like to think that a partial answer, at least, may be found in the comment of former Deputy-Under Secretary of State Robert D. Murphy before a recent conference of broadcasters:

"You, as communicators in the open society we cherish, provide the vital and selective liaison between governments and people, people and events, events and ideas . . . You are reporting, influencing and actually making history . . . If peace does finally come to the world it will be largely due to the fact that mass communications have played a major role in this great effort."

CREDITS: Magnum Photos (*Eve Arnold, Brian Brake, H. Cartier-Bresson, Dan Budnik, Rene Burri, Cornell Capa, Bruce Davidson, Elliott Erwitt, Burton Glinn, Ernst Haas, Erich Hartmann, Bob Henriques, Wayne Miller, Inge Morath, Marc Riboud, John Fell Stevenson, Dennis Stock*); CBS Photos (*Irving Haberman*); Wide World Photos; Press and Information Office, Federal Republic of Germany; British Information Services

22453